Lee Milteer's
Five Types
of Energy

T0145471

UNIVERSAL SECRETS FOR MANIFESTING SUCCESS

FREE BONUS

Five Types of Energy Video Series for Our Readers

Each energy video is about five minutes long.

FREE video series to help you use your life energy more effectively:

WWW.FIVETYPESOFENERGY.COM

Sign up for this FREE video series to learn about your five types of energy!

Video One: Mental Energy

Video Two: Emotional Energy

Video Three: Financial Energy

Video Four: Physical Energy

Video Five: Spiritual Energy

Praise for *Activate Your Inner Power* and Lee Milteer

Concise. To the point. Candid. Clear. Two hundred and fourteen (!) answers to 214 vexing problems, challenges to autonomy, and recurring obstacles to confidence and power. A coach in a book. When confronted with a "dragon," go to this book's table of contents, and go directly to exactly the right "sword." *Activate Your Inner Power* is as useful a desktop reference for peak personal performance as the thesaurus is for the writer or advertising copywriter.

—Dan S. Kennedy
Author, NO B.S. *book series, business strategist and serial entrepreneur*

Brilliant! Go ahead and test it. Think of a question or just ask for inspiration. Then open the book. Instant wisdom! I love it!

—Dr. Joe Vitale
Author, Zero Limits; The Miracle

Having known Lee Milteer for decades, I have seen the impact she delivers to the world. The insights she shares in this book are powerful and effective to help anyone spark a journey of transformation in life. I always say that people should stop thinking about mindset and should start thinking about mind growth. So, from one impactor to another: Lee, you have created an inspiring resource of mind growth for your readers!

—Mike Agugliaro
Author and coach

Lee Milteer has a unique way of bringing great clarity in ways that no one else can. In this powerful book, she takes you by the hand and guides you in finding your life's purpose with her easy-to-implement steps. This book is highly recommended for anyone who feels stuck, doesn't know what their life's destiny is, or is looking for a life of deeper meaning.

—Monica Main
Author, The Lost Secret

The biggest determinant of success is how determined you are to have it. Lee's book is chock full of wisdom and insights that will guide you to new solutions for age-old problems. If you are determined to have a better life, let this book be your shepherd.

—Mike Michalowicz
Author, Profit First; Clockwork; Get Different

So many times we have questions for ourselves on how to live our life and on decisions we should make. On one side we know what we want to do, and on the other side we doubt ourselves, or we let other people's input stop us from believing in ourselves. In *Activate Your Inner Power*, Lee Milteer helps you focus on those specific areas in your life where you have questions for yourself, and she helps you tap into your intuition to answer them. Lee shares specific information that guides you to find answers to the challenges you face. We often don't trust our own intuition and what we already know to be true. This easy-to-read and easy-to-use book will give you the courage to believe in yourself and the power to manifest a better life for yourself. It won't be long before my copy is dog-eared.

—Roslyn Rozbruch
President, Tax & Business Solutions Academy®

Activate Your Inner Power by Lee Milteer is the embodiment of using your intuition and natural instincts to find guidance and direction in the very confusing world we live in. This book trains your mind to seek another perspective and view of your challenges and to take the high road verse falling back into fear and doubt. This book is a must for people you love to help them find themselves in life during these challenging times.

—Ben Gay, III
Author, The Closers

As a huge fan of Lee Milteer's wisdom and advanced knowledge on mindset, practical spirituality, and overcoming huge obstacles in life, her new book, *Activate Your Inner Power*, lives up to its title. This book activates you to call forth your own internal personal power by giving you suggestions, tips, and new ways to see old problems and challenges. This book empowers you to claim your own sovereignty and stop giving away your power to others who might not have your best interest at heart. This book will literally reduce your stress and worries about the outside world by activating within you the answers and guidance you need at this time.

—Debbie Allen
Bestselling author of ten books, the world's #1 authority on expert positioning

Finally! An illuminating book for anyone searching for answers in today's complex world. *Activate Your Inner Power* by Lee Milteer contains over two hundred wisdom-filled pages offering specific business, relationship, and wealth-building advice to successfully navigate the obstacles that are holding you back from success. This amazing resource is now my trusted go-to guide, offering action plans with each message that are clear and concise. All you need to do is follow them! You'll be amazed at the accuracy and truth of each message as your intuition and inner powers guide you to the appropriate page selection!

—Lily Noon
President and CEO, Noon International, Inc.

If you've felt stress, fear, doubt, or insecurity with the changes happening in today's business climate, Lee Milteer's new book, Active Your Inner Power, is the ultimate resource to get back on track. Lee's insightful statements, stories, and solution-oriented action items will help you overcome confusion and gain clarity to even your most perplexing challenge. These bite-sized, easy to apply strategies will help you reempower yourself to get the results you seek now. I found tremendous value from the myriad of topics and insights Lee teaches in this book and highly recommend it. If you are seeking answers to confusing questions and want clear, concise action on what you should do, get this book now and start benefiting from its powerful advice.

—James Karl Butler
Best-selling author, Clear and Present Game Changers; The System is the Secret

Success is an inside job. The six inches between your ears has unlimited potential if you learn to leverage it correctly. Lee's amazing book *Activate Your Inner Power* will coach you to do this with simple steps. When you read this book and act on the numerous strategies and tactics Lee shares, you will encounter a level of success and significance that is truly extraordinary!

—David Bush
Coach, Extraordinary Results

Lee Milteer's latest book, *Activate Your Inner Power*, is no theoretical "self-help" book. Lee has been in the trenches with what works in the real world, day in day out, to help entrepreneurs and individuals from all walks of life really live their best life. Her techniques and strategies will help you thrive in all areas of your life whether professional or personal. This book has my highest recommendation and will be immediately distributed to all my family members and clients.

—Stephen Oliver, MBA
Ninth degree Black Belt, Business coach and consultant

Activate Your Inner Power is both a spiritual book and a workbook that is perfectly designed for our times. Each page is filled with wisdom that jumps out at you. Then Lee provides guidance on how to bring manifest that wisdom into your life.

I especially like how this book teaches how to unlock and activate our intuition in order to serve us best.

It is a book that is timeless and is the gift you keep giving yourself each time you open it.

—Jeffrey Deckman
International award-winning author, Developing the Conscious Leadership Mindset for the 21st Century

Lee's book should be titled When the Student Is Ready the Teacher Will Appear. That teacher is Lee Milteer. Lee is one of the best mindset, heart-set, practice business, and spiritual teachers in our world, and has delivered processes for people to find guidance within themselves in this upside down world to know the best routes to take with confidence.

—Ryan Kussner
Entrepreneur

Can this book actually provide you with useful, actionable, practical advice no matter what you are facing by merely thinking about the issue and then turning to a purely random page?

Or is it truly "random"? Are there unseen forces working on our behalf, helping us, guiding us?

The "force," collective consciousness, the universal mind, infinite intelligence, God force—call it what you will. Lee has spent her entire career learning about, experimenting with, and distilling this concept down to its very essence and then explaining in plain, easy to understand terms these unseen forces of nature and how they work.

Release your inhibitions, open your mind to the "what if" inside you that deep down wants to believe. Try it for yourself. Test it. Then clean off a special place on your bookshelf of go-to books. It really is that good.

—Jesse S. Lennon III
Investor and developer; President, Pioneer Realty

Lee Milteer does it again with her newest book, *Activate Your Inner Power*. This gem of a book sits at my bedside, and every night—just before sleep—I randomly flip to a page for inspiration. Lee's words activate my subconscious to help me create the life in my dreams and, in turn, of my dreams! The action plans guide me to execute on my goals to create a life of prosperity. The universe seems to conspire in my favor when I activate my inner power!

—Thie C.L. Convery, B.Sc. (Hons), R.F.P., CFP, CIM, FMA, FCSI
Wealth advisor

In Lee's timely new book, *Activate Your Inner Power*, you get profound nuggets of advice and guidance to help you deal with and function more effectively in a sped up, digital, and fear-based world. We often forget to get advice from trusted advisors and to also rely on our internal God-gifted compass system known as intuition. Get this book. Read it as needed. Apply it when called upon and let it percolate in your mind and heart to achieve a life of greater fulfillment.

—Tony Rubleski
Bestselling author and consultant

It's been said that when the student is ready the teacher will appear. The reason the teacher "appears" at just the right time is because eventually most people reach a point of desperation, exhaustion, and sometimes heart-breaking frustration because they're not getting their life to where it needs to be.

Lee's new book, *Activate Your Inner Power*, is composed of 214 powerful nuggets of wisdom to inspire you to play a bigger game. The fun thing about Lee's book is that you need not read it in order. At any given moment, you can pick it up, flip to any page and see what pearls of wisdom Lee has to share. I'll bet you'll say to yourself, "I wonder how Lee knew exactly what message I needed today?" Enjoy *Activate Your Inner Power* and if you haven't yet, be sure to get a copy of Lee's brilliant mindset book, Success is an Inside Job—you'll thank me later!

—Cap't Jim Palmer
The Dream Business Coach

This book is a stunningly simple and graceful reminder that there is a world of answers out there if you would simply search for them. Far too many of us lose direction without consulting available resources that can help us not only turn the corner, but to thrive and succeed beyond our wildest dreams. If you want to find the answer to any question, ask, ask, ask!

Lee Milteer's brilliant road map serves to guide the reader on a journey of not only self-discovery, but to rev up the engine of inquisitiveness so that questions asked, and answers found, propel the reader to action and movement.

Bravo Lee—another wonderful addition to our worldwide library of superb personal development literature!

—Rodger Friedman
Retirement wealth manager; Author

Activate Your Inner Power is just another example in Lee Milteer's long list of achievements that shares her deep knowledge and insightful wisdom about peak performance and excelling in our chaotic world of confusion, disconnect, and distraction.

This book is uniquely structured so that the reader can navigate simply and easily to any pearl of wisdom that they desire.

The focused topics are all easily digestible and include an action plan so that the reader can implement the concept they are reading about and get immediate results.

Whether you start at the beginning and read straight through from the beginning to the end, or whether you jump around and focus on the topics you happen to be interested in, the list is long and there is something for literally everyone.

The wisdom of "Amp Up Your Superpowers" really resonated with me. We are all endowed by our creator with a set of superpowers that are uniquely our own. Discovering and using these superpowers for good can be used to define a person's unique purpose in life and can give you direction and guidance that will last for a lifetime.

Keep this book by your bed so that you can digest a pearl of wisdom when you wake up in the morning and when you drift off to sleep at night.

Miss a meal if you must, miss a television program if you must, but don't miss *Activate Your Inner Power* by peak performance coach Lee Milteer. You will thank yourself now and in the future.

—Robert Olsen, CPA
Founder and president, The Robert Olsen Wealth Group

ACTIVATE YOUR INNER
POWER

ACTIVATE YOUR INNER
POWER

———•———

A Book of
Guidance Messages

———•———

LEE MILTEER

Copyright © 2022 by Lee Milteer.

All rights reserved. No part of this book may be used or reproduced in any manner whatsoever without prior written consent of the author, except as provided by the United States of America copyright law.

Published by Advantage, Charleston, South Carolina.
Member of Advantage Media.

ADVANTAGE is a registered trademark, and the Advantage colophon is a trademark of Advantage Media Group, Inc.

Printed in the United States of America.

10 9 8 7 6 5 4 3 2 1

ISBN: 978-1-64225-734-2 (Paperback)
ISBN: 978-1-64225-733-5 (eBook)

LCCN: 2022919012

Cover design by Jivan Dave.
Layout design by Analisa Smith.

This publication is designed to provide accurate and authoritative information in regard to the subject matter covered. It is sold with the understanding that the publisher is not engaged in rendering legal, accounting, or other professional services. If legal advice or other expert assistance is required, the services of a competent professional person should be sought.

Advantage Media helps busy entrepreneurs, CEOs, and leaders write and publish a book to grow their business and become the authority in their field. Advantage authors comprise an exclusive community of industry professionals, idea-makers, and thought leaders. Do you have a book idea or manuscript for consideration? We would love to hear from you at **AdvantageMedia.com**.

Hold a Problem in Your Mind,

Open This Book to Any Page,

and There Will Be Your Answer.

CONTENTS

Why I Wrote This Book

Activate Your Inner Power is about you consulting with your *inner power*—a part of you that is connected to Infinite Intelligence. You were born with an inherent birthright to this inner power, where your instincts, intuition, and guidance system reside. You accessing your own inner power is not in the interest of society, educational systems, religions, and governments who want to control you to maintain the structures of *their* systems.

Sadly, we have been taught since birth that we need others to guide and advise us on important matters. We must free ourselves from these limiting mental constructs and claim our original wholeness with our inner truth and nature. You have within you many resources, talents, and skills that go unused or undeveloped because the outside world is programming you to not trust yourself.

I learned the secret of how to gain wisdom by consulting with my inner power (which I call my higher self) when I was twelve years old. I was dealing with some adult challenges and my father, a self-educated rancher/farmer, shared with me the surprising thing he did when he felt lost, confused, and indecisive.

A big reader, he showed me how he would go to his small library of books, sit in front of them, and ask which book would give him the answers to his dilemma. He would just look at the books until one popped out to him energetically and got his attention. Then he would hold the book and ask again for the answer to his dilemma. He would open the book to the place he felt inspired to open and start to read. He assured me he always found solace and inspiration from this exercise.

If this information had not come from my own father, I would have laughed at it since nothing in my life had given me any hint that I had these abilities.

After he left me in the room with his books, I picked a book, opened it at random, and started to read.

To my shock, the best advice just found me. I stared in amazement at the page that now was giving me some comfort and perspective. This one technique has helped guide me personally through some tough life storms when my motivation was gone, and I felt like giving up.

I have personally taught this incredible inner power secret in my books, at Vision Quest retreats, and at business coaching and speaking events around the world. We are all connected and have access to a great spiritual life force. Your job is to move away from distractions, fears, and doubts and sincerely ask for help, fully intending to receive an answer.

Be prepared! Answers can come from many places, so pay attention: they can come from the book you are holding, from a conversation you hear, or in a TV show or movie. Just know if you *ask*, you have alerted your conscious and subconscious mind to find an answer. Your subconscious mind has recorded everything you have ever heard, seen, and learned since the minute you were born. It is now looking for the answer you are requesting. Tip: focus on the solutions you want and not just the "problem."

I have used this "find the answer" technique when feeling unresourceful, sad, or confused and the positive pattern interrupt technique always lifts me up. It's the greatest pattern interrupt ever! It has helped me find the perfect aligned topic to enlighten audiences at speaking events. I also use this technique when I need inspiration writing books and articles and dealing with daily challenges.

Picking any guidance message page in this book will distract you positively and also can be an effective diffuser. Anytime you consult with your inner power by the simple act of opening this book to any page at random, it will start to shift your experience, guiding your attention away from self-pity, despair, confusion, and inner distress.

When presented with difficulties, know that your soul is reaching out to grow and expand. If you ignore the difficulties, they will continuously show up again and again, just with different names and at different places. Learning to trust your own instincts and intuitions will give you great confidence, perseverance, strength, and discernment.

Consider this book a guide that can reframe your view of your own life. When you shift your mind, you shift your life on your own unique journey! When the student is ready, the teacher appears and the teacher is your inner guidance system.

Introduction

Consulting Instructions to Use This Book

The purpose of this book is to activate a point of contact connecting you with your own inner guidance—to start a conversation with that inner part of you that can remove stress, fear, doubts, and insecurity when you need truth to help you make the best choices and actions.

Ask and You Will Receive

Picture in your mind a problem you are grappling with. Ask for your inner, secret power to give you— right now—a fresh perspective, inspiration, and guidance.

Take a deep breath and hold it. Think on your problem once again, ask for guidance, and then release your breath. Open this book to any page at random and there will be guidance messages to help you find an answer to your challenge. (If you are reading a digital version of this book, simply ask your inner power what page number and then go to that page.)

Be open minded and just allow whatever message you receive to be considered. The simple act of *asking* your inner being for a solution engages your inner power to assist you with messages that will lead you to seeing the situation from a new perspective with a new mindset.

All challenges are opportunities for learning and creating a new reality. By shifting your perspective and consciousness, you get a new view of it and where hidden opportunities might be.

Suggestions to Benefit from This Book

You may want to simply read this book from start to finish to seed your conscious mind and subconscious mind with the messages in this guidebook. Just reading this book at any page is designed to reset your mind to a different vibrational energy, offering you new perspectives and options that will lead to new opportunities you have not acknowledged before.

Pattern Interrupt—If You Are Having a Bad Day

Open this book to any page at random to find a new message to focus on. Or you can scan the table of contents for a possible title that may be the exact page you are seeking for guidance. Since you literally can only think one thought at a time, the message you find will help your inner power shift your mind and attention to more empowering, nourishing, and productive thoughts. This will interrupt any pattern of negative, energy-draining self-talk making you feel fearful, insecure, angry, frustrated, resentful, retaliatory, or depressed. A pattern interrupt will restore the flow of your creativity, clarity, and discernment.

You might write down affirmations or intentions resulting from your new mind shift and conspicuously post them places to remind your subconscious mind of the progress you have made.

What If You Cannot Relate to the Message You Got?

Think of life as an adventure! If you open to a page that simply doesn't resonate, feel free to ask again and open to a new page until you feel you have a message that resonates with you. Or look at the table of contents for a theme that you feel attracted to read. You may well find multiple page turns will bring your mind shift into sharper focus!

There is no limit to how you communicate with yourself. The purpose of this book is to offer you a point of contact connecting you with your own inner guidance.

First, the quality of your messages and guidance depends on the focus and clarity of your question. Make sure you are asking your questions in the following framework:

* ❊ What am I to learn from this situation or see in an entirely new perspective?

* ❊ What guidance message could help me with what I need to know today?

❋ Where do I need to shift my energy and focus to take back my personal power right now?

❋ How could I take a message I don't relate to and consider new frames of reference?

The point of *Activate Your Inner Power* is that you get *guidance* directly from a higher source. You have your own spirit guides, guardian angels, spiritual helpers, Infinite Intelligence, or God in the invisible realm and, since this is a free-will planet, you have to *ask* for help. Just like in the Bible where it says, "Ask and you will receive."

Activate Your Inner Power is about *you* living *your* life with the powerful benefits of inner guidance. So, no matter how hard the challenges or how big the stumbling blocks, this book will be here to encourage and help you make the shift your self-esteem, mindset, motivation, and direction needs.

Making the right decision is a universal worry. Any time you have to decide with only partial information, you are ripe for the stress of "rightness" worry. This form of anxiety is particularly debilitating because of its prolonged duration. Even after making decisions, you may deal with anxiety and second-guessing yourself.

When Dealing with Fear, Doubt, and Insecurity

Now you have something specific you can do that works in minutes. You can use this book to immediately start to calm yourself physiologically and mentally. Simply open this book to any page at random, read, and you will set your wheels of guidance in motion.

Take Action

Your greatest growth results from facing your fears and taking actions toward your desires and goals. Simply taking physical action at the beginning of your goal quest helps you get the momentum and confidence that will assist you in achieving your dreams.

You have much more power than you ever imagined, and you have unlimited potential to manifest your unique destiny and outcomes. All you have to do is *trust* yourself and take your callings and dreams seriously. This is your life, and you have an obligation to give yourself all the support possible to achieve mastery in the areas you are called to.

Using this book can help you re-empower yourself by rewiring your brain to suit the information that you feed into it. When you are constantly searching for opportunities, abundance, love, and reasons to be grateful, you will find it much easier to attract the positive things you are focusing on with your mind and emotions.

Taking the time to ask for your inner power to give you guidance is a form of self-comforting. Yes, taking charge of the caliber of information that you feed your mind and becoming proactive about taking action toward the future you really want is a very powerful way to reshape your reality and future.

Consider this book a personal guide that can reframe your view of your own life and work. When you shift your mind, you shift your life. When used to connect with your personal inner power, this book can literally open doors of new opportunities, prosperity, and peace of mind in every area of your life.

Your point of power in this life is this very minute in time. *Ask* for a message and receive one—but from that moment you must take some action toward the outcome you desire. You must be proactive toward that which you desire.

Suggestion

Keep a journal of questions and answers you get. Use this written record to confidently remind yourself that you can indeed "activate your inner power" to live the incredible life you want!

Bonus for You

Please find at the back of the book three prayers for you (the prayer for direction and guidance, the prayer for goal-driven behaviors, and the prayer for visionary insights) from my book *The Magic of Prayers* to assist you in finding your own guidance messages. Enjoy!

Blessings, love, and magic to you!

Lee Milteer

www.milteer.com

1

Facing Old Challenges

Still facing old challenges that stand between you and your dreams? To overcome your challenges, you need to create goals, of course, which are easy to write down.

The real work is in the preparation that needs to happen before you can reach your goals. This requires great self-discipline. It is the power of discipline that will carry you across the finish line.

Action Plan

Answer this fast before you have time to think about it: What disciplines are you creating now that will take you where you want to be? Don't forget to write them down! Take action toward at least one thing ASAP.

2

You Are the Decider

Imagine you have a blank canvas on which you can paint your life and business masterpiece. Having a theme for the year, a written vision for your life, and goals are the fundamental tools—the paint and brushes—you need to create your personal work of art.

You must prepare yourself for the times of struggle, sadness, and frustration that will surely come … but there will also be celebrations, victories, and happy surprises.

Action Plan

You can't control everything that will happen to you, but you can control how you respond to what happens. Get started today since "someday" is an illusion that will put a tombstone on your dreams.

3

Every Single Morning of Our Life, No Exceptions

We get a chance to be different.

A chance to change.

A chance to be better.

Your past is your past. Leave it there. Get on with your future now. You are about to walk into the *best* year of your life if you are willing to change your habits and focus. You have the power to be whatever you are willing to create.

Action Plan

Shake things up and get out of your old routines today. Celebrate when you do this, because you will be taking the first step into the *best* time of your life! Expect miracles!

4

Your Self-Talk

Don't be a victim of *negative self-talk*. Remember, you are listening.

Without exception, you are a self-fulfilling prophecy. So, become very aware of your internal and external talk, because it is the roadmap to your future.

If you think you can or think you cannot, you are correct!

Action Plan

Keep tabs on what you are saying to yourself, so you can remove any self-talk sabotage. Remove words that sabotage you, such as "trying," "wanting," "can't," and "needing." These words put you in a victim mentality.

5

Get Clear on Your Goals and Dreams

Knowing what you want should be first on the list because your energy, thoughts, and focus will dictate how everything else shows up for you.

Action Plan

Make your energy, attitude, and mindset a priority. Create systems to ensure that your dominant thoughts are in alignment with the ideal reality you want to manifest. Act as if your dreams are already yours now! Go for the life you want.

6

Say "No" at Appropriate Times

Be aware of your people-pleasing past—when someone asked you to do something and you immediately responded, "Sure!"

Action Plan

Instead, respond to such requests using one of these magic phrases: "I have to check my calendar" or "I have to think about it."

Consider filtering every request with these important questions: "Does this fit what goals I have now for my life or work?" and "Is this something I want to do?"

More specifically, consider your relationship goals, work goals, financial goals, and goals for physical, emotional, and spiritual health. If the request doesn't advance you to where you want to be, politely decline.

Learning to say "no" at appropriate times will take some getting used to on your part, but the payoff will be substantial because, maybe for the first time in your life, you are using your life energy toward your inner directions versus just trying to do things to please others. Please make yourself a priority because your life aspirations are important too!

7

You Only Get a Limited Time on Earth

Make it a good day to do something you are proud of and something that contributes to *your* personal goals.

Action Plan

Put your goals up in places you can see them daily, such as your refrigerator, personal bathroom mirror, or closet. Know that what you can see finds its way into your subconscious mind, which works 24-7 to expand what you're focused on.

I will do it tomorrow is a lie because we never know our departure date, so make today count.

8

The Future Is like a Blank Book

Today is your chance to write a new, beautiful story for yourself. If you don't pick up your pen and write your own story down, someone else will happily write it for you, using all your energy in directions that are not beneficial to you.

Action Plan

If you are not scripting your goals daily, you are missing your chance to tell Infinite Intelligence what life you want to live. Write a story about your future self and how much fun and great your life is, how healthy you are, how your relationships are thriving, and how you feel so blessed with prosperity.

9

Habits That Must Be Retired

What habits are no longer working for you and should be retired?

They could include any of the following:

❋ A habit that doesn't feel fun anymore

❋ A habit that doesn't make you healthier

❋ A habit that doesn't bring out the best in you

❋ A habit that doesn't elevate your impact

❋ A habit that doesn't make each day better than the last

❋ A habit that doesn't strengthen your relationships

❋ A habit that doesn't bring more wealth into your world

* A habit that doesn't make you a better leader

* A habit that doesn't make you more loving toward yourself and others

* A habit that, in all honesty, you just don't have time or space for anymore

Action Plan

Write those old habits down that you need to release and post them so you can privately be reminded every day to create better habits to take the place of the old habits you wish to replace. Don't fight the old negative habit, just substitute a new action or behavior in place of the nonbeneficial old habit. In a short time, the new behavior will take the place of the old behaviors and you will be free of that burden.

10

Go in the Direction of Your Dreams

To change your life, you need to change your priorities.

It is time to be a bit selfish for your own soul's journey. You have a purpose within you to fulfill, and only you can do that. End your procrastination and your fear of getting started by taking action. Just take baby steps, which will lead to big steps.

Action Plan

Get clear about who or what you have allowed to hold you back from going in the direction your soul urges you to explore. Then start. Give yourself permission to experiment with living your own calling, and trust yourself to be able to figure it out.

It is better to make mistakes than never go for your secret desires.

11

"Stop Doing" List

Sometimes you need a "stop doing" list as badly as you need a "to-do" list.

If you don't break your cycle of self-injury from your own bad habits, no one will do it for you. Step up to the plate and be good to yourself.

Action Plan

Get out of denial and tell yourself the truth. There is no time like right now to send your conscious and subconscious mind directions to stop doing the things that cause you pain and unhappiness. Give yourself new, beneficial directions on how to use your life energy.

12

Belief Prisons

You are *confined* only by the walls you build yourself. You hold the key to the prison you are in. Why aren't you questioning some of your old beliefs about how life should be? Are these beliefs actually yours, or are they ones you have inherited from society, school, your family, or your church?

Break free from the past. The past is over, and you have a grand future ahead of you if you are willing to let go of what is no longer working for you.

Action Plan

Give yourself permission to let go of beliefs and behaviors that keep you from being your true self. The past is gone, so let it go.

13

Call Back Your Energy

Call back the energy you have lost by worrying or having anxiety about how other people may perceive you. Use that energy to rebuild your inner peace by deciding to love and accept yourself as you are right now, flaws and all. It will radically improve your life.

Action Plan

Control your thoughts, control your life.

14

Detachment Mindset

Detachment doesn't mean not caring. It means taking care of yourself first and letting others take responsibility for their actions without trying to save or punish them.

Action Plan

Stop saving people from themselves. Sometimes you must let them fall on their faces—failure is part of everyone's learning process. No more rescuing people who are capable of learning tasks they pretend to not be able to do, or people who refuse to learn after repeating the same mistakes over and over.

15

Wear Your Invisible Crown

Wear Your invisible crowns, kings and queens of the world!

If you don't crown yourself, no one is going to recognize your right to be your own, sovereign self.

Action Plan

Celebrate your life more. Enjoy everything in your life and stop waiting to celebrate! Wear your nice clothes before they go out of style or dry rot, use your good china and silver, burn those nice candles, and use the good towels and soap! Why wait for your relatives to inherit them? Claim your life and your right to a beautiful life by using your resources, time, and life your way!

16

Let It Hurt, but Then Let It Heal

Focus on your healing, and never let anything that happens to you turn you bitter.

Action Plan

Let it go. You can't change what happened, but you can choose to not let it change you.

Don't let betrayal, people revealing themselves, disappointment, and pain define you. You are bigger than that. You are never how someone makes you feel. Let it hurt, then let it heal … but don't linger there. Remember who you are and rise and move on with your head held high.

Let it hurt, but then let it heal. Find love in your heart, forgive, let go, and move on. It's the only way to truly end your suffering.

17

Love Is Always the Answer

Action Plan

The pathway to love is forgiveness.

Forgiveness dissolves resentment.

Take the time to recognize exactly who and what you have not forgiven.

Now forgive them so you will be free.

The gift of forgiveness is meant for your benefit, not for the person you are forgiving. Know that forgiveness is a process where you don't "forget" what happened; you just don't let it rule you anymore.

Sometimes you must forgive someone repeatedly to completely dissolve your feelings of resentment. Love yourself enough to be free from the past. Value your present so much that you are not willing to allow the past to imprison you.

18

Your Year of Discipline

Decide this is your time for true success discipline.

Decide what you want.

Write it down.

Make a plan.

Work on it every single day!

Your competition isn't other people; it's your procrastination. Compete against that.

Action Plan

Conquer yourself by creating discipline in the areas you want to improve and watch miracles happen to your productivity and happiness.

19

Impact Your Future

There are three big *C*s of life:

- ❋ Choices

- ❋ Chances

- ❋ Changes

You must make a choice to take a chance, or your life will never change.

Action Plan

Decide on some new choices today that will impact your future.

Be bold, be visionary, and be wise to make new choices, give yourself new chances, and experience new transformational changes.

20

Take More Risks

If you want to double your success rate, all you have to do is double your failure rate by taking more risks.

Action Plan

Just do it! Go for your dreams—the worst thing that can happen is you improve on your plans. Think of life as an adventure and everything as an experiment. Nothing ventured, nothing gained. Go for life!

21

Your Point of Power Is Right Now

The past cannot be changed, and your future is in your power to influence yourself.

Action Plan

Stay in the present, which is your gift to manifest.

Do not let worry or doubt hold you back from right now taking new actions and seeing life from new perspectives. Seed your mind with empowering data and keep yourself motivated by focusing on exactly what you want to create for your future. Your Imagination is your only limit.

22

Never Regret a Day of Your Life

Good days give happiness, bad days give experience, worst days give lessons, and the best days give memories.

Action Plan

Everyone and everything has made you the strong, resourceful person you are today. You needed it all to make you the masterpiece you are now.

23

Walk Boldly past Obstacles

Most of your obstacles would melt away if, instead of letting them stop you, you made up your mind to walk boldly through them toward the life you desire.

Action Plan

Reprogram yourself to see that obstacles are just the realization of the next step you must take to get to your better future. If you don't overcome the obstacle on your first try, you are always free to keep trying until you do. Be brave and have courage to never let any obstacle best you!

24

Manifesting Mindset or Victim Mindset?

Action Plan

Ask yourself, "Am I playing to win or merely playing *not* to lose?"

Your honest answer will make it clear what road you're currently on. You must play to win—and expect to win. Seed your mind and environment with positive symbols, uplifting messages, and signs of prosperity.

You choose your intentions and mindset daily.

Reveal to yourself where you are playing not to lose. Claim what you are now going to do to play to win! Remember it is your game, so you get to choose how you play!

25

Become a Manifester

Become a powerful manifester through gratitude. Please remember:

* ❋ Your job is the dream of the unemployed.

* ❋ Your house is the dream of the homeless.

* ❋ Your smile is the dream of the depressed.

* ❋ Your health is the dream of those who are sick.

Beautiful things happen when you distance yourself from negativity and fearful thoughts.

Action Plan

Feeling grateful puts you in a manifesting attraction mode. Write a list of everything you are grateful for, focus your energy on being grateful, and watch your life shift into a better place.

26

Life Is a Gift

You are not promised tomorrow.

Action Plan

Do the things you want to do today.

Include little things, like writing love notes to your sweethearts and notes of appreciation to those people you are glad to have in your life.

Tell people you love them. Make it a habit to tell them how much they mean to you.

Enjoy the now, for it will only be a memory in the future.

Make a list of things you have been putting off for a tomorrow that may or may not come.

Pick one thing off the list to do today. Celebrate now!

Today is your power!

27

What Is the Worst That Can Happen?

If you're really unhappy with an area of your life, it's up to *you* to be brave enough to fix it. Take some risks and make some changes.

If you need some motivation to help you set some needed changes in motion, ask yourself, "What is the worst that can happen?"

❋ People will be unhappy with you.

❋ You will fail, despite your best efforts.

So what? No doubt you have stepped on a few toes before and maybe crashed and burned before. But that was then, and you need changes made now.

Action Plan

Gather what you can learn from your past mistakes, and attempt again to secure the life you want to enjoy. Go for your life upgrade!

28

Things That Don't Define You

Here are some things that don't define you:

- ❈ What others think or say about you
- ❈ Your past mistakes
- ❈ Who you used to be
- ❈ Your relationships
- ❈ Your profession, business, or job
- ❈ Past traumatic events and situations

Action Plan

Put your life into perspective with these old perceptions of yourself. That was the past. Today is a new day! Release the things that don't define you and embrace a life that you love. Every day you wake up presents a new opportunity to be a better you. Don't let the past prevent you from a great future! Your future story has not been written yet. You get to write this new story about *you*!

29

Deliberately Attract Abundance

Action Plan

Invite great, new, positive energy into your life. Prepare to receive the love, good fortune, and miraculous opportunities that are meant for you. Use this prayer whenever you feel unresourceful.

ABUNDANCE PRAYER

I am now releasing all negative energies that have seeped into my life. I let go of cynical belief systems, unhealthy habits, negative behaviors, disappointments, regret, revenge, anger, and grudges. May the flushing of all this from my being attract to me all the goodness I am aligned with. So be it.

30

Use Your Life Energy Wisely

Catch yourself if you find you are carrying your mistakes around with you in your head, replaying them over and over. This just programs your brain to make the same mistakes again and ruins your day.

Action Plan

Use your mistakes as stepping stones under your feet, marking your path away from your past blunders and miscalculations. Let your mistakes provide the important lessons you need to move forward in some area of your life. Never lose hope for yourself and your future. If it is meant to be, it will be up to you! Give yourself permission to learn from mistakes and come up with better solutions.

31

Make a Firm Commitment

The first step toward getting somewhere is to make a firm commitment you are not going to stay where you are now.

Action Plan

The best part about getting back on your feet is knowing who and what you are not going to walk with again. Sometimes you have to be done. Not mad, not upset. Just done. Now you can move on in your life to new adventures.

32

Take Some Time Off

Most of us wish someone would say, "You need some time off, so take your life and enjoy it." So say it to yourself. Say, **"You deserve to enjoy being alive. Take charge of your life and time and enjoy it."**

Action Plan

Pick a day or week to relax. If you don't, your body will pick it for you.

Life is not about working all the time. Balance your life and plan some time off. Everyone needs R & R to rejuvenate their energy and creativity. If you don't schedule the time off, you will not get it. Make yourself a priority and take care of your mental and physical health. Invest in yourself with this time off by doing fun, creative, and restful things, so you can go back to your life refreshed and rejuvenated.

33

Life Is Literally Happening for You

Nothing in life has happened to you. It's happened for you.

Every wrong, disappointment, and betrayal, and even every shut door, have helped build you into the strong person you are today.

Action Plan

Forgive all the characters in your life's play who played the bad guy role. They were life teachers. Now that you have learned the life lessons, you can release them. Once you release them, you can see how they helped you move to a different perspective.

34

Relationship Survival Tips

You need to come to terms with some facts of life:

* People are going to let you down.

* People are not going to see life the way you do.

* No response is a response.

* If they wanted to, they would.

* Not everyone has the same light and heart as you.

* Not everyone will be honest or take the high road.

Action Plan

Don't take what others do so hard. Their behavior is a reflection of who they are, not who you are! Love and appreciate yourself so much that what *they* do is not important.

35

Amp Up Your Superpowers

This is a personal reminder:

❋ You are powerful beyond measure.

❋ You are capable of pretty much anything you are willing to work for.

❋ You have determination, grit, and perseverance for all your core passions.

Action Plan

Take positive action to amp up your superpowers.

Envision surprising the hell out of those who doubt your potential and what fun that will be! Have fun using your confidence at full power to attract new adventures, fun, and profits!

You are as powerful as you allow yourself to be!

36

Addicted to Drama?

An unhealed person can find offense in almost anything someone does. Most people are addicted to their suffering and therefore constantly in conflict with the world. It is the ego's way to maintain power. A healed person understands that the actions of others have absolutely nothing to do with them.

Action Plan

Each day, you get to decide which one you will be— healed and free or unhealed and nursing old wounds. Take nothing personal since what others do reflects themselves and not you. Inner peace begins when you choose not to allow another person or event to control your emotions. Your mind is a powerful tool. When you fill it with positive, nurturing thoughts, your life will reflect what you focus on.

37

Action Is the Cure

Action is the cure for many of your mind problems. Most of your obstacles will fade away when you make up your mind to just walk boldly through them.

Depression goes away when you make a decision and a clear plan and follow through with action. Indecision disappears once you have started down a clear path.

Often, the right people and situations seem to appear when you shift your energy from staying on the fence to having a clear plan of action and the fortitude to carry it out.

Action Plan

Make a list of the things with profit potential that you've been putting off doing. Pick at least one action, be brave, and take some profitable actions today.

Actions remove depression!

38

A Reminder in Case Your Mind Is Playing Tricks on You Today: You Matter

You are loved and important. Your presence on this earth makes a difference, whether you see it or not. You have some special abilities, talents, and skills that only you can share with the world.

Action Plan

You really do matter in this world, so treat yourself like you do!

The truth is if you do not value yourself, no one else will!

39

Learn Your Limits

If you're a *giver*, remember to learn your limits because the *takers* don't have any! Remember that zebras do not change their stripes!

Action Plan

Your job is to protect and maintain your own life energy and not allow vampires to feast on you. Give up rescuing others since that is not your job.

Stay away from users and abusers! Give them the gift of your absence!

40

Utilizing Your Own Life Energy

Think about how much self-care time you are spending on the following:

* ❋ Yourself

* ❋ Going for your goals and ambitions

* ❋ Enjoying your hobbies

* ❋ Sharing time with loved ones

* ❋ Taking care of your health and well-being

What books, podcasts, newsletters, and business clubs are you absorbing that are empowering and inspiring you to be your best?

What new knowledge are you applying in your daily life and work?

Action Plan

Always be investing time in yourself since it is the most lucrative investment you can ever make.

Your return on this personal improvement and self-development investment will always be beneficial and pay off in great dividends.

41

Get Out of Denial!

When it's time to make a change, the world will clearly make your life so uncomfortable that you will have no other options but to change. When you are not happy or not thriving in a situation, don't stay in denial, ignoring all the red flags.

Action Plan

Reframe yourself! The world has better plans for you, so trust in the process and do your part by aligning yourself with the things you want. Releasing what is not working for you opens up new opportunities for your life to upgrade.

42

You Can Never Go Back to What Was

That door is closed and now only a memory.

Action Plan

You can only start from where you are now. Gather yourself up and start taking those steps toward the future you want to experience. Start to *act* as if what you want is already in your current reality.

If you want to be rich, act rich and stop saving "nice things" for only celebrations. Every day should be celebrated!

If you want to be healthy, start doing the things healthy people do.

If you want a great friend, become a great friend.

If you want to write a book, sit in front of the computer at the same time every day and write!

You can only start from where you are now.

Start manifesting. Today is the first day in your new future. Make it a good one.

Your future is in your hands.

43

Instincts Are Messages to Keep You Safe

Here are some valuable lessons to never forget:

❋ Your brain understands facts.

❋ Your heart understands emotions.

❋ Your intuition understands truth.

Action Plan

Pay attention to the whispers of truth; write them down. Above all, follow your intuition. It will tell you everything you need to know. Your instincts are messages to keep you safe. Allow your intuition to help guide you in all your decision making.

44

Your Spiritual Frequency

Anyone who is not on your same evolutionary and spiritual frequency will distance themselves from you, while all those who are on the same frequency as you will become more connected to you.

Action Plan

Don't take it personally when people wander away. It just means they are on a different evolutionary track than you. Be OK with that fact. Wish souls Godspeed. Let them go to learn their own life/soul lessons!

45

Reframe Your Life

Action Plan

Learn to deal with troublesome annoyances by working with them and reframing the meanings. View what is happening that is currently troublesome as a neutral observer who isn't privy to all the natural forces at work.

For example, say a traffic jam threatens to make you late for an appointment. Think: maybe the Universe is saving me from some awful accident down the road.

Life is how you frame it. Frame it with you in charge since your only power in life is how you choose to label things and the attitude you decide to have in any situation.

46

You Are Never Stuck!

Life changes every single moment. You want to change the way things are? Change your thoughts to the way you want things to be. You have manifesting power in the energy of your thoughts.

Action Plan

Never assume that you are stuck with the way things are right now.

Believe in yourself! The ticket to your most happy life is in your head! Envision the change you want to see in your world and start looking for solutions to bring that change into reality.

Change your mind, and you change your life. You always deserve to give yourself another chance!

47

Difficult Events Make You Stronger

Action Plan

Accept that every single event and situation in your life—especially the difficult ones—have made you stronger and wiser than you were before. Consider all the challenging situations and difficult people in your life as *gifts* that teach you determination, courage, grit, and resiliency!

Allow others to live their own truth—even if it's completely opposite from yours—without shutting off your compassion for them. It will be a beautiful reflection of how powerful your love is and what a good soul you have developed in your life.

48

Celebrate More!

Please do not wait until you have reached your goal to be proud of yourself. When you celebrate, you vibrate at a higher frequency, and that is an attractor for you to bring more blessings and joy into your life.

Action Plan

Embrace every step you take to reach your goals and become the person you are today with a big smile and a sense of accomplishment that will propel you to your next step. The more you celebrate your progress, the more progress you will enjoy!

49

Think Bigger—Pull the Trigger

Are you scared to go for what you deeply want? Sometimes we dare to think of big goals and then get scared away from doing anything about them. That vision that feels too big for you wouldn't be in your awareness if you weren't already fully equipped to achieve it. You were born to do great things with your life.

Action Plan

Think bigger. Pull the trigger on your goals, knowing everything you want is already created and you are just catching up to the goal.

50

Give Yourself Peace

Honestly, your peace is more important than driving yourself crazy trying to understand why something happened the way it did. **Learn what you can from mistakes, certainly, but also learn at what point you need to let them go.**

Action Plan

Forgive yourself for whatever part you played, and forgive the other players. Let this situation go completely so you can be set free to move on in your journey of life. Just let all your past go. Free yourself from the burdens of yesterday's mistakes and know you learned great lessons, so the experience added value to your life.

51

How Strong Is Your Mind?

You must train your mind to be stronger than your emotions or feelings or else you will lose yourself and your personal power every time.

Action Plan

When you feel triggered to respond to a situation in a nonbeneficial way, pause and ask yourself, "What is my second response here that I will feel better about later?"

You may have to go to your third or fourth chosen response in your mind before you respond in real life. And don't forget, sometimes not responding is the best path to take. Just let the situation pass on by and pay it no mind.

The important thing is that you don't get triggered to lose your temper and say words that might be forgiven but never forgotten. Self-control is the highest control you can have in life.

52

Reap What You Sow in Life

You will always reap what you sow in life; it's a law of life.

Action Plan

If you are not receiving exactly what you want in life, change your strategy and start to be more of what you want to experience.

Be kind

Be fair

Be honest

Be generous

Be forgiving

Be true,

and all these things will come back to you. Sow what you want to reap in life.

53

There Are No Perfect Times

Life will never be perfect. Don't wait until everything is just right before jumping into action toward exactly what you want. Life is always giving us challenges, obstacles, and less than perfect conditions. So what?

Action Plan

Do it anyway!

Whatever endeavor is on your heart, create a plan and get started now. With every action you take, you will grow stronger and more skilled, more self-confident, and more successful. All energy gets results. You have no control over external circumstances and the twists and turns life takes, but you do have control over your intentions and dedication to fully live life to its full potential.

If you ask a tree expert when the best time to plant a tree is, they will say, "Twenty years ago." But when is the next best time to plant a tree? *Right now*!

Right now is your true power!

54

Follow Your Own Heart's Calling

Don't let other people's opinions slow you down, cause you frustration, or cause you to lower your own belief in yourself.

Keep in mind some people have to pretend you're a bad person, so they don't feel guilty about the things they did to you.

Accept reality:

1. You'll never please everyone. Some people just love to find fault; it makes them feel superior.

2. They don't know where you've been ... or where you're going.

3. Their opinion is mostly about them ... not you.

4. Critics never matter.

Action Plan

It's your life and your aspirations that are important. Focus on your own inner callings and intuition about how to live your own life. See the beauty around you. Break out of your boundaries. Reach out to what makes your life more meaningful.

Ignore other people's opinions and follow your own heart. This is your life, after all, so what difference do other people's opinions have with what your soul is calling you to experience?

55

Ten Things Mentally Strong People Do

1. They embrace change, focusing on what they want, not what they don't want.

2. They welcome challenges and are willing to take risks.

3. They move on and don't waste time feeling sorry for themselves or holding grudges and anger.

4. They control their emotions and moods and focus on what they can control.

5. They choose to be kind and fair and honor their own word.

6. They speak up for truth and justice.

7. They celebrate other people's success and are happy for them.

8. They're grateful for what they have in life and focus on being happy.

9. They are the givers of life, and love being of service and helping others.

10. They plan their life and work their plan.

Action Plan

Create a plan to incorporate these attitudes into your daily life.

56

Release the Wrong People Currently in Your Life

Life is just too short to be anything but happy.

Action Plan

The right things start to happen when the wrong people leave your life.

Here are four ways to hasten their exit:

1. Walk away from all the drama and the people who create it.

2. Surround yourself with people who make you feel loved, honored, and appreciated.

3. Laugh more and worry less.

4. Love the people who treat you right, and pray for the ones who don't.

Removing what is not supporting you and what is causing you unhealthy stress and unhappiness opens doors to new energy and opportunities. Remove the old and replace it with positive supportive energy. Yes, this takes some courage and fortitude, but the rewards will be worth the effort of removing what is not working in your life to make room for what can work!

57

Honor Your Personal Word

Your personal word means everything. If you break your word, not only will others not trust you, but you will also lose self-confidence and not trust yourself.

Action Plan

Say what you mean and mean what you say with your words and actions. If you give someone your word, do everything in your power to keep it. If you cannot, immediately renegotiate and make new commitments. Your life depends on you honoring your own words. Remember your brain is listening to you and acting on what you are saying to yourself. Stop letting yourself down.

58

Strength Doesn't Come from What You Can Do

Strength and fortitude come from overcoming the things you once thought you couldn't do.

Action Plan

Think of all the things in life you thought you could never do but did.

Write down what your self-talk is currently telling you that you cannot do.

Break that negative spell coming from your own insecure internal self-talk and start to proclaim that you have the abilities, determination, dedication, and persistence needed to accomplish big goals. Reinforce and acknowledge to yourself daily that you are going to do it anyway because you are that strong!

59

Self-Talk: The New Approach to Self-Care

Most people's internal self-talk dialogue is over 80 percent negative. If you're like most people, then you could benefit from making some internal thought changes. You are a self-fulfilling prophecy, after all.

Action Plan

Consider a new strategy and start talking to yourself today with the same loving words you use with your loved ones or your sweet, four-legged furry companions: "Hey sweetie! Look at how beautiful you are. You are so smart; I love you so much."

Bottom line: Start to talk to yourself like you care about this person (*you*) and want to support them in their dreams and endeavors with internal messages of motivation, inspiration, and uplifting messages. Talk to yourself like you would your best friend.

60

Life Is Not Happening to You; Life Is Happening for You

It might take a day, or it might take a year, but what's meant to be will always find its way to you if you are open to it and actively going toward your goals.

Action Plan

Know that what is meant for you will come. Keep working and dreaming for the life you want to experience. Be open minded—what is meant for you could show up in a package that you might not expect.

Look for the good in life in every situation.

Also know that people and things that leave your life are moving you to a new place to continue your soul journey—to where you are supposed to be. Don't mourn what is gone; simply look for the new adventure. Life is always moving you toward your best outcomes. We do have to let go of the old to attract new, more aligned people and situations.

61

No Rule That Says You Have to Live Life like Everyone Else

Action Plan

Live your own adventure. Be honestly true to yourself; it's your only real obligation in life. Let go of the fears and doubts that say you must conform to whatever is happening in the world right now. You are a sovereign being, and that means you get to decide what is for your own highest and best good in your own life.

62

Be Smarter with Your Communications

Get out of old, insensitive communications habits. Important conversations are best done in person, where your tone of voice can be heard, facial expressions seen, and energy felt. Be aware that your words and deeds can forever alter the trust and relationships between you and the people in your life.

Action Plan

Train yourself to stop texting and emailing important communications. Become more human in your kindness, compassion, and sensitivity toward your fellow human beings. Keep in mind that what you sow in communications and energy is what you receive.

We need more compassion energy in this world.

63

Be Aligned with the Future You Want

If it doesn't make you feel great and aligned with who you are right now, follow this advice:

1. Don't do it.

2. Don't buy it.

3. Don't keep it.

Feeling fat, frumpy, outdated, and old? Well, it's time to shed that old image! Give yourself permission to have your style, which is whatever it is that makes you feel like the unique soul you are!

Remove all things in your home, office, and closets that simply are not you anymore; you have evolved! Accept that you are no longer available to things and people that make you feel bad.

Action Plan

Become more aware of what you feel about situations, things, and even your clothes. When you get dressed, be aware: how does this outfit make you feel?

Your goal is to feel good. Get rid of "things" that don't live up to this promise. Release traditions and old routines that simply have no meaning to you and replace them with activities that bring you inner peace and joy.

Life is short, so live your best life, and only you can give yourself permission to do that!

64

Be the Change You Want to See in the World

You cannot force someone to hear a message they are not ready to receive. But you must never underestimate the power of planting a seed of knowledge and being a good example.

Action Plan

Be the change you want to see in the world. Be the example of wisdom, kindness, compassion, and good common sense. Your example is much more powerful than your words. Be the calm in the storm. Be unattached to what others do and think and more aware of what energy you are sowing in the world. Being a good example is your best solution in all situations.

65

Be Compassionate

If we had the ability to investigate the lives of others, to peek into their hearts and minds, we would see and understand the hardships they face every day.

If we take the approach of compassion, we will treat each other with more kindness, patience, tolerance, and sensitivity.

Action Plan

Never assume you have a clue what is going on in people's lives. When you need clarity, ask questions, but treat others like you would like to be treated. The golden rule is always your best guidepost.

66

I Am a Work in Progress

The work I do on myself is not a goal; it is a process—a lifetime process.

Action Plan

Choose to enjoy the process and all the life lessons. Remember you co-create the process with your thoughts and actions. Be kind and loving to yourself because every day is a new day to be a better person.

67

Nothing Changes until You Do

Here are six realities you need to accept:

1. Your weight is a reflection of your daily habits.
2. Your wealth is a reflection of your daily habits.
3. Your mood is a reflection of your daily habits.
4. Ninety percent of the problems in your life are *your* fault.
5. Excuses won't solve anything.
6. Life is not always fair.

Action Plan

Clean up your act, and clean up your life.

Give up past excuses, get yourself an accountability partner or coach, and create sustainable new habits that cure your old problems. Nothing changes until you do.

Today is a great day to start to make positive changes. Success is truly an inside job first.

68

Choose Your Perceptions Wisely

Some people could be gifted baskets of roses and only see the thorns. Others could be given a simple weed and only see the beauty of its tiny flowers.

Perception is the key component to gratitude. Those who have trouble getting past the sharp thorns of the roses have no gratitude for the gift. Those who discover the weed's little flowers are full of gratitude for their gift.

Gratitude is the key component to joy.

The baskets of roses bring no joy to those who have no gratitude for them. The simple weed brings great joy to those who are grateful for it.

Action Plan

Take a personal perception inventory: Are you more likely to see thorns or flowers in the things life presents to you?

Keep in mind that what we perceive—what we focus on—always expands. You can enjoy a more joyful life when you choose your perceptions wisely. Decide you are going to look for the good wherever possible. Decide that the negative perceptions you used to have now are no longer welcome, and you will decide to create the habit of seeing blessings in all aspects of your life.

69

Creating Yourself

Life isn't about finding yourself. Life is about reinventing and upgrading yourself. Be the good you want to see in the world and leave a good example of love. The world needs more good people.

Action Plan

※ Don't give up on the future.

※ Keep fighting for the good.

※ Keep showing up and being a good soul.

※ Keep having compassion and being kind.

※ Keep being brave and trying new things.

※ Keep caring and giving back.

※ Keep showing grace and *be* the light you were born to be!

70

Time Is What You Make It

Time is measured by your feelings, decisions, and psychological condition—not by clocks.

❋ Time is slow when you wait.

❋ Time is fast when you are late.

❋ Time nearly stops when you are sad or bored.

❋ Time speeds up when you are happy.

Action Plan

Choose to have a nice time and enjoy yourself no matter what. You can be happy waiting at the airport or for an appointment if you intend to be in the now and enjoy it. Since you cannot replace your time, use it with awareness. Your time is one of your most precious resources, so don't squander it away being in unresourceful moods.

71

Happiness Secret

The secret to being happy and content is to accept being in the now. Accept where you are in life, and make the most out of every day.

You can look back on your life at the things you feared and worried about and realize that you worried and fretted for nothing. Life has a way of working things out.

Action Plan

Focus on your blessings more and less on what makes you unhappy. What you are grateful for will always multiply. Focus on the small blessings, such as who you love and who loves you. We can decide to be happy and let the bad habit of feeling unhappy fade away. We are the ones who make ourselves happy or miserable over the labels and definitions we assign to events. Wake up daily with the clear intention that today is a great day. Look for evidence of your blessings. Change your mind, and that will change your life. You have the ability to choose to be happy and ignore the rest.

72

Who Cares What People Think of You?

When you're a teenager, you worry about what everybody is thinking about you. When you're 45, you don't care what anybody thinks about you. When you're 65, you realize nobody's been thinking about you at all.

People spend their days worrying and thinking about themselves and their problems, not about you. The most important cage you can free yourself from is the one in which you care what others think of you. Life is short, and you must think of yourself and what you want and need.

Action Plan

Live your life the way *you* want. It is your life and your future!

73

Release the Job of Rescuing People

One of the greatest awakenings that will shift your life and energy is when you realize that not everybody changes or wants to change. Some people never change. That is their journey. Accept that it is not your job to try to "fix" them.

Action Plan

Devote your time and energy to taking care of yourself and do not get sidetracked using your life energy to fix other people's problems who have no intention of changing their behaviors. Save yourself and just focus on what improvements you can do for yourself. Give up all your *rescue* behaviors unless you are asked for advice or help. You are interfering with their own soul's learning lessons when you take them on as a rehabilitation project. Plus, if you fix their problems, they will not learn their own life lessons and will have other challenging situations come up again and again until they learn on their own. Give yourself permission to allow others to deal with their own self-created challenges.

74

Stop Explaining Yourself to People

Life is so much simpler and happier when you just do what works for you.

Action Plan

Give yourself permission to let your authentic self out! It is your life and *your* adventure, so live it your way. No need to explain yourself. Just decide to live happily ever after!

75

Self-Judgment

Sometimes you glimpse in the mirror and see a mess when you look at yourself. At that moment of self-judgment, you don't see the lives you've touched or the people you have helped. You don't see all the love and kindness you've given freely. You don't see the shining example of a good human being you have been. You forget about your extraordinary courage to face all your challenges. You don't see your bravery standing up for those you love. You forget all the extraordinary memories you've made.

Action Plan

Take more time to acknowledge and appreciate yourself. You are a spiritual being in a human body and your job is to live your life being of service. Love yourself and release self-judgment since you are a work in progress.

76

Reinforce the Good

You never know how much pain, fear, doubt, and emotional agony others are experiencing.

You never know how much someone needed that smile or thumbs up you gave them.

You never know how much your encouragement turned someone's entire life around.

You never know the true impact you have on those around you.

Action Plan

Be a light in someone else's life. Your gestures of caring may give them the strength to keep going.

77

Just Keep Moving Forward

When you feel stressed, take a step back, take a deep breath, and laugh. Remember who you are and why you're here. You're never given anything in this world that you cannot handle. Be strong, be flexible, love yourself, and find a way to love others.

Action Plan

Just keep moving forward. Small steps create great adventures! Great things can manifest when you are looking for them. Do some self-care, walk in nature, play with your animal companions, watch a funny video, or read something that comforts you to pattern interrupt the current stressful time. Keep in mind that you can only think one thought at a time. Why not choose better thoughts? Change your focus, change your mind, and thus change your moods.

78

You Gotta Stop Watering Dead Plants

Stop pretending you are happy in certain situations when you are truly miserable, such as in a dead-end job or a dead-end relationship. Stop pretending certain people are real friends when, clearly, they are no longer showing you any proof of that.

Do not be fooled: A person's most consistent behavior is their true self. Period.

Action Plan

Notice when you literally can feel your energy being drained when you're around people you shouldn't be around. This is a very strong indication to remove yourself from these vampire energies. When you allow the wrong people and situations to leave your life, the right people and things start to appear.

79

Your Dream in Life Doesn't Come with an Expiration Date

Your chances for success are enhanced with every consistent, forward-moving attempt you make toward that dream, since you will have more resources from what you have learned. All worthy dreams take time, energy, and resources.

Action Plan

Ask yourself: Are you investing time, energy, and resources into your dream that you want out of it? Take a deep breath and try again with a better plan of action.

80

What You Focus On Always Expands in Your Life and World

Anything you think about repeatedly affects your feelings, imprints upon your subconscious mind, and becomes a part of your personality. Your mind is a fertile garden; seed it wisely with uplifting thoughts.

Action Plan

Think about what wonderful adventures you want to experience and enjoy in your life. Focus on what is good to make sure you are giving your brain the correct directions to create the future you want. Immerse yourself in education and the wisdom of a good coach or mentor to keep you on track. Connecting with people who have taken the journey you want to take is invaluable to cut down on the headwinds.

81

This Isn't Serving Me

It's so empowering to claim, "This isn't serving me." Don't try to swim against the current by wasting your life energy on people and situations you cannot change! You'll only wear yourself out and then get carried downstream anyway.

Action Plan

Give yourself permission to release all unresourceful situations, relationships, and old mental and emotional baggage such as grudges, resentments, and anger. Give yourself and the world a pardon and free yourself from negative energy drains. Releasing what is no longer yours to carry is a great gift to give yourself.

82

You Must Love Yourself First

Society has not taught this to us, but you must love yourself *first* because no amount of love from others is sufficient to fill the yearning your soul requires from you.

Action Plan

Say loving things to yourself, and imagine yourself feeling loved, honored, and appreciated. Emotionally, your body doesn't know the difference between an experience and a thought, so you can literally change your biology, neural-circuitry, chemistry, hormones, and genes with such daily self-care.

Add to that spending time in nature or with your four-legged fur babies or anything that brings you true joy. Success is an inside job that only you can create. You can only love others to the extent that you have the capacity to love your own flawed human self. Only when you accept yourself can you accept others. It is an act of courage to finally lay down the wounds of the past and just claim the right to love yourself right now, no matter what happened in the past.

Today you must claim the innate power of love within you. Self-love will be the greatest gift you can give your soul and the one gift that will reap the highest rewards to your life.

83

Give Up Fear of the Unknown

We as humans are afraid of not knowing what comes next, so we make our lives predictable, hoping to avoid pain. We give away our power to so-called experts, which costs us time, money, and, often, our health.

Action Plan

Don't be afraid of what comes next.

You have always landed on your feet, and you will again.

Write this down: You'll be okay. Go on with life.

You are writing your own story, so make it a good one.

84

Quit Right Now

Fearing change means a few things:

* ❋ Living in the past
* ❋ Trying to please everyone
* ❋ Putting yourself down
* ❋ Overthinking
* ❋ Following the herd of others and what they do

Action Plan

Be over all the self-sabotage of all of the above. Unless you make a new decision and take new actions, you are going to stay exactly where you are now, programming your mind and body with detrimental thought and action patterns.

Be willing to change, willing to have an open mind, and super willing to take new perspectives of what is possible in life now. Then start taking some actions in the direction of your new habits. Repetition is the key to making new, positive habits stick.

85

Just Be Your Real Self

No matter what other people think or say, Infinite Intelligence made you the way you are for a reason.

Besides, an original is always worth more than a copy!

Action Plan

Break free from the constraints of other people's programming and belief systems.

When things are out of your control, your worry, fear, and doubt will only make matters worse.

Let go of your insecurity that you are not good enough.

Let go of your fear that you will not be perfect.

Embrace yourself with new possibilities.

86

Become the Best Version of Yourself

Fall in *love* with the process of becoming the very best version of yourself by reinventing yourself and giving yourself permission to create a brand-new, updated version of you—a version of you that is filled with optimism, renewed creativity, and excitement about life's possibilities. The new version of you has the visionary abilities to see opportunities that you can leverage and monetize. It's your life story, so write it with great discernment.

Action Plan

Starting something new or making changes requires serious effort, persistence, and inner motivation. Doubt, fear, and worry impede your progress and keep you stuck. Intend to do your best right now, envision the end results you want, and act as if you are exactly as you want to be! Magic will happen for you when you go in the direction of being the best version of you!

87

Your Diet Is Not Only What You Eat

Your diet is what you watch, what you listen to, what you read, who you associate with, who you allow to influence you, and what environmental factors you are around.

Action Plan

Become fierce of who and what you allow in your environment and mind and who you associate with. Pay attention to what you feed your soul, not just your stomach. The caliber of information and the caliber of people you allow in your life will determine the quality of life you will experience.

88

We All Have Complicated Pasts

We've all made some choices and decisions that clearly were not the best, but we were doing what we could at the time with the knowledge and information we had. Clearly none of us are completely innocent, but the good news is we get a fresh start every single day to be a better person than we were yesterday. Life is about learning and growth! Forgive and move on.

Action Plan

The past is a closed door. Learn from it and move on with your life. Improve some part of yourself every day! The only person you are in competition with is the person you were yesterday.

89

Beware of Distractions

If you don't separate yourself from your distractions, your distractions will separate you from the life you desire.

Action Plan

Acknowledge what distractions are keeping you from achieving your goals. Get some assistance from someone who can truly help you create the perseverance, discipline, and clear plans to move past these destructive, time-sucking distractions that currently hold you back from your true potential.

90

You Shine Too Bright for Some People

Some people are going to reject you because you shine too brightly for them. Don't be sad. It is OK since they don't pay your light bill! It is their choice to be intimidated.

You are an original—live up to that! Write those books, speak your truth, play with your artwork, create your successful business and family, and have the adventure of your life!

Action Plan

Keep shining your personal light everywhere you go and with everything you do. It is not your problem; you shine bright!

91

Be Independent in Your Thinking and Actions

Never let yourself be controlled by the following:

1. People
2. Money
3. Your past
4. Fear
5. Herd mentality
6. What society is doing
7. Past programing
8. Confusion

Action Plan

The past is a closed door; the future is only in your imagination, and your true power is *right now*, in the present. Start living your true life right now. It is your life, by the way. You are supposed to make the rules.

92

Never Speak Negatively about Yourself

Even if you're speaking in jest, your subconscious mind doesn't know the difference. Words are energy patterns and cast spells—that's why it is called spelling!

Action Plan

Change the way you speak about yourself, and you will change your life in dramatic ways.

You are a self-fulfilling prophecy so upgrade your language skills to speak to yourself in ways that your subconscious mind will get the programming of who you are becoming.

Head's up: if you are not deliberately changing, you are choosing to stay the same.

93

Confidence

You glow differently when your confidence is fueled by your own belief in yourself instead of validation from the outside world and others.

Action Plan

Stop holding on to your unworthiness. Give it up and see what a worthy human you are. Decide to reinstall your self-esteem and self-worth by surrounding yourself with information that supports you and your quest in life.

94

Your Relationship with Yourself

Your relationship with yourself sets the tone for every other relationship you have.

Today is the day to set a new tone of love and self-respect for yourself, which, in turn, will affect all the other relationships in your life. The more you honor yourself, the more others will honor you.

Action Plan

Take the time to do the following:

* ❋ Love yourself.
* ❋ Respect yourself.
* ❋ Admire yourself.
* ❋ Forgive yourself.
* ❋ Nurture yourself.
* ❋ Give yourself another chance.
* ❋ Look for the positive.

95

Rejection

Rejection can be hard, but there is great consolation in knowing when you're chasing the wrong people or things; in fact, that is when rejection becomes a *huge* blessing.

Action Plan

Learn to value rejection just as much as you value direction. Know some things are just not for you, and it is a blessing you were rejected.

Say this simple prayer when entering a new venture:

Dear Infinite Intelligence, please show me right away if this _____ is not for my highest, best good, so I can focus my energy elsewhere in a more productive way. I ask for guidance and direction for my highest and best good for myself and all concerned.

96

Take Care of Yourself First

Sometimes you get so busy helping others you forget that you're important, too. If you don't take care of yourself first, you will burn yourself out and be depleted. Once you are no longer resourceful, you will not have the resources to assist others.

Action Plan

Before saying "yes" to others, make sure you are not saying "no" to yourself. Pause before accepting invitations and ask yourself, "Is this action good for me? Will I be happy? Will there be a fair exchange of energy? Or will I be the giver of energy and they will be the takers?" Having clear discernment will always help you make the right decisions at the right time.

97

Discerning When to Share Knowledge

You can give a person knowledge, but you can't make them think. Some people want to remain uneducated, or in denial, because the truth may require them to change when they don't want to change. Change is scary to them, and they want predictability. Like the anonymous quote says, "The truth has no defense against a fool determined to believe a lie."

Action Plan

Don't get upset anymore once you realize who you are talking to. Be glad you just got a better understanding of who you are dealing with and can now make the proper adjustments (like no longer wasting your time and breath!). It is not your job to fix them.

98

Self-Mastery Is Training Your Mind to Be Stronger than Your Emotions

Fail to train your mind to be stronger than your emotions, and you'll lose yourself every time.

Action Plan

Build a strong mind. Your mind is a garden; your thoughts are the seeds. You can grow flowers, or you can grow weeds. It is always your choice. What are you focusing on?

Emotions are like storm clouds that pass through your mind and body, and you can control your thoughts, which will control your emotions. It is always a good idea to spend time in nature and contemplation in order to connect deeply with yourself and your true intentions.

99

Be Thankful

Being in gratitude will feed your courage and determination.

When you wake up in the morning, be thankful. Be thankful for the life that you have, the roof over your head, and the food you eat. Be thankful for your family and friends, staff, coworkers, and customers. Remember to hold your loved ones and even your four-legged fur babies a little tighter, stay a little longer, and tell them you love them and why you love them.

Action Plan

It's important to let them know you appreciate *who* they are and acknowledge what contributions they make to your life.

Have fun with a 30-day sticky note campaign.

Here's how:

Grab a pad of sticky notes and write some fast "I love you" and "I appreciate you for _____" (fill in the blank) notes to your kids, partners, and family, and even to your *team* at work. Watch this one gesture gain so much traction with them. You'll probably see them showing you love in return. Have fun. The sillier you are, the better!

100

Expectation Is the Source of All Suffering

Peace of mind is the result of programming your mind to accept life for what it is right now, rather than longing for what you want it to be.

Action Plan

Be in the now. We must retrain our mind and emotions to be more neutral and not have attachments. Life has a way of working out details you could never have imagined.

101

Your Past No Longer Defines You

Say the following statements out loud:

- ❋ I am not my childhood trauma.
- ❋ I am not my high school or college trauma.
- ❋ I am not my parents or siblings.
- ❋ I am not my ex-relationships or old friends.
- ❋ I am not my failures and the poor choices I have made.
- ❋ I am not the victim.
- ❋ My past no longer defines me.
- ❋ I have the power to grow, learn, and heal from anything and anyone in my life.
- ❋ I get to decide and define who I am.
- ❋ I get to write my own story.

Action Plan

Daily script your new story so your future will be seeded with new adventures and happiness. Your story is waiting to be written by you. Your past should be viewed from the lens of what you learn and how life has always guided you when you listened to your intuition for the right directions for you.

102

Stop Waiting for Apologies and Move On

Most apologies are never going to arrive. You only torture yourself by hoping and waiting for them. The truth is that wounds you pick at never heal.

Action Plan

The best revenge is to live your very best life by moving on, forgiving, and letting the person or situation completely go. Free yourself from your expectations and suffering. Live your *best* life no matter what others have done or said. Forgive them for your peace of mind and close that chapter and forget it.

103

The Real Measure of Your Wealth

The real measure of your wealth is how much you'd be worth if you lost all your money and position.

Action Plan

What is your creativity, loyalty, dedication, persistence, imagination, fierce work ethic, love, friendship, integrity, perseverance, grit, kindness, generosity, and the ability to start again worth?

Everything!

Fear nothing since within you are all the tools you need to navigate in a new place.

104

Action Cures Depression

If you rearrange the letters in the word *depression*, you can spell "I pressed on."

Your current situation is not your final destination by a long shot.

It is the beginning of a new adventure.

Action Plan

Take concise, intelligent action on something as soon as possible. Action cures depression. It moves your mind from feeling lack to a feeling of moving forward.

105

Nothing Is by Chance

There are no coincidences or accidents in the world. Everything you're experiencing is a direct manifestation of where you're focusing your energy, your attention, and consciousness. Nothing is by chance, so are you paying attention?

Action Plan

When you are impacted by coincidences or accidents, ask yourself, "What does this mean?" and examine your intuition on it. What is Infinite Intelligence trying to show or tell you? Are there patterns of things you are ignoring? Pay attention! Your own higher self is doing its best to communicate with you. Don't blow these events off as insignificant. In particular, ignoring red flags will cost you later! Train yourself to be aware.

106

Give Yourself a Break!

Sometimes the kindest thing you can do for your heart and soul is to let go of the burdens that you were never meant to carry. You can pray for solutions, but you cannot carry burdens meant for others who have the resources and tools to deal with those problems.

Action Plan

If there is a problem and you personally have literally no way to solve it, then it is *not* your job to try to fix it. You can pray for the highest and best outcome for all concerned. Send them love and do whatever small thing you can do to add light to the situation. Just do not carry that which is not yours to carry.

107

Give Up Arguing with People

In life, it's important to know when to *stop* arguing with people and simply let them be wrong.

Action Plan

Save your breath, control your ego, and realize some people are just very young souls who are not going to have the ability to discern truth like you. Give them the gift of your absence when they are in argumentative moods. Be a good example of love and integrity by allowing people to make their own decisions and deal with those decisions. You must take the high road and let people believe whatever they want.

108

Get Up Again

Stop being ashamed of how many times you've fallen … Start being proud of how many times you've gotten up again.

Be proud of the adversities you have conquered, the evil you have resisted, and the times you took the high road.

Action Plan

Life is about your choice of thoughts and decisions. Decide to be proud of your ability to learn and personally grow from all of your experiences. Life is about growing into a more conscious human and continuing to get up again.

109

Become Your Own Biggest Fan

Consistency is harder when no one is clapping and rooting for you.

You must clap and support yourself during these times.

Action Plan

You must always be your own biggest fan and be proud of your resilience and grit. Envision your dreams as already in reality and know that you have an inner guidance that is always encouraging, clapping, and rooting for you.

110

Welcome Change

You can change the trajectory of your life by programming yourself to welcome change.

Say daily to yourself:

✳ I am now releasing all things from my past that have caused any negative attachments and pain.

✳ I prepare and welcome new changes and new adventures.

✳ I welcome new opportunities to grow mentally, emotionally, spiritually, and physically that are for my highest and best good.

Action Plan

Identify your opportunities. Act toward those opportunities; writing them down counts as the first action. Actions make things happen. Look for opportunities, and you will find them.

111

Hold Space

Sometimes the best you can do is be the light In someone else's darkness today.

You cannot solve others' problems, but you can encourage them, suggest solutions, and be the voice of reason, hug, and smile they need. Hold space for them when they are having a hard time.

Action Plan

Just allow your intuition to guide you. Pause before responding to people's problems and ask yourself, "Exactly what could I offer at this moment to assist that empowers them?" Learn not to take responsibility for others' predicaments.

You can, if they are receptive, offer them the frame of mind and some solutions they could enact on to tackle the challenge.

Remember, if you solve others' problems before they learn the lesson, you keep them from learning to take risks and think for themselves. So be the light of encouragement!

112

Practicing Discipline

Successful people achieve their success by simply practicing discipline every day. This is true in any profession, athletic or entrepreneurial.

Action Plan

Write down the names of the disciplines you are not practicing daily but that would up your game to achieve any type of goal—from losing weight to dropping a bad habit and improving your relationship with yourself and others.

Often, avoiding routine means you get very little accomplished. Disciplined consistency is the big secret to *all* success.

113

Some People Will Never Volunteer to Change

A truth that you must awaken to is that not everyone wants to change, and some will never change.

They have decided to stay as they are. That is their right and free will to do. It is not your job or journey to try to fix them to your view of life.

Action Plan

Trying to change people who don't want to change is a futile act. Awaken to your real job—to first take care of yourself and pay attention to your own journey.

Accept people where they are. Ask yourself, "What level of consciousness or stage of their life is this person in?" and allow them to learn their own soul's lessons. You don't have to pour energy where it is not welcomed. Go where you are appreciated and valued to offer your help!

114

Have Faith in Yourself

What is yours is going to find its way to you.

Your purpose in life can only be found by you.

Action Plan

Be sure you are daily seeding your mind and emotions with positive, optimistic thoughts about the future, such as, "My life is getting better and better daily in exponential ways; positive opportunities and miracles always happen for me."

Claim your desires daily with your self-talk, intentions, and focused deliberate actions toward your personal aspirations. Have a plan of action to execute daily so your destiny finds you faster! No matter what, decide to believe in your own abilities.

115

Let the Past Go

Never let the past define you ever again! Give it no more energy and the "problem" will fade away from your consciousness from lack of attention.

Action Plan

Make a choice today that the following "situations" will no longer define you:

- ❋ Current bad news

- ❋ Past trauma

- ❋ Your body

- ❋ Your family

- ❋ Your relationships

- ❋ Your education or lack of

- ❋ Your job, career/profession

❋ Mistakes you have made in the past

❋ Where you came from

❋ What people say or think about you

Today is a new day to start a new phase of your life where your old self is no longer judging you. This is your one life, so enjoy it.

116

The Power of Risk-Taking

If you are serious about steaming ahead toward the dreams you sincerely want, you must take risks that most others would not take.

"It's *impossible*," says your pride.

"It's *risky*," says your past experience.

"It's *pointless*," says your head.

"Give it a try," whispers your heart.

Action Plan

Make up your mind to walk boldly through your obstacles. Most of them will melt away when you take intelligent action. Nothing ventured, nothing gained.

117

Fair Exchange of Value

If you are a giver, you must also be a receiver. Remember to learn your limits because the takers of life don't have any limits and will gladly suck you completely dry and come back for more.

Action Plan

You must be accountable to yourself with an awareness of fair exchange of value. If you are always the giver, your well will go dry without it being replenished. Your relationships become unbalanced, and this is not healthy for you. Stop accommodating people who don't prioritize you. Release the takers and gift them with the absence of you. You will then receive the best energy possible when you nurture and take care of yourself as a priority.

118

Head, Heart, Gut Decisions

Here are some lessons to integrate into your daily life to make valuable decisions:

❋ Your brain understands facts and past programming.

❋ Your heart understands emotions and feelings.

❋ Your intuition discerns and understands *truth*.

Action Plan

When making *choices*, review all your head/heart/gut data.

That inner knowledge (intuition/gut reaction) will tell you everything you need to know if you ask and are open to the truth.

Your instincts are a message from your inner being (your soul) and are the greatest bridge to your spiritual growth and inner peace.

119

Your Inner Journey

The path to transform the quality of your life is an inner journey. No one can do it for you. If you are tired of reacting to life, choose different responses to life's insanity.

Action Plan

Become a neutral observer of your life's situations, particularly the unfortunate ones. Then simply accept them, without the whining victim self-talk. Whatever the situation, view it as if you had chosen it to happen.

This will help you creatively reframe the situation so you can turn it to your advantage in some way. Work with the energy field you are in, making the energy your friend and ally, not your adversary. How creative can you be in looking at the situation from a different lens and looking for some good you could benefit from? This new action will exponentially transform your entire reality and life.

120

Success Is an Inside Job

You have the map to your most rewarding life already inside of you now.

Believe in yourself and act as if everything is going to work out because it is going to work out.

You have landed on your feet before.

You are going to land on your feet again and again.

Action Plan

Focus on exactly what you want your future to look like.

Envision it with a vision board.

Script it out in meticulous detail.

Expect it to come to you with perfect timing.

Talk about it; immerse yourself in your new future and life, knowing and believing that your life is going to thrive in all ways because *you* are going to make sure it does!

Your new affirmation is, "I always wind up on *top*! Everything I touch turns to gold."

You are a self-fulfilling prophecy. This is your story … Write a good one!

121

Act "As If"

Become the best version of yourself today.

Simply become the person you want to be. Embody the behaviors, actions, and mindset of the real person you desire to be.

Action Plan

A proven way to reprogram your mind is to simply act "as if." You must first be able to expect yourself to upgrade.

Start to think, act, and walk in alignment with being that upgraded, better version of yourself.

As you continue to Act "as if," your nervous system and brain will reprogram itself to identify with your new choices, which turn into habits.

122

You Are Your Only Limit

Until you understand this fact of life, you will blame your education, society, religion, family, friends, bosses, kids, past, etc. for holding you back.

Action Plan

Follow the four simple rules in life:

1. Take 100 percent responsibility for your past, present, and future.

2. If you don't go after what you want, you'll never have it.

3. If you don't ask, the answer is always no.

4. If you don't move forward by taking intelligent, planned risks, you'll stay stuck where you are. The distance between your dreams and reality is measured by your action.

123

Never Taking Anything or Anyone Personally

Stop taking things personally and get your personal power back!

Action Plan

1. Take the mental and emotional position that other people's unkind, self-centered, rude, dismissive, condescending behaviors *are not about you*. Their behaviors reflect who they are. Notice how they treat other people with the same disregard as they have treated you.

2. When others make comments or criticisms, have a curious mindset. Ask yourself the constructive question, "If there is any truth to what they have

offered, is there something I can learn from this feedback?"

3. Look at others' negative behaviors toward you from a different perspective. Ask yourself how an unbiased bystander would view the situation.

4. Accept that you simply cannot please everyone. Some people defy gravity with their expectations.

5. Realize that you are not defined by your human mistakes or other people's disapproval.

6. Take your personal power back by realizing that your self-worth and high self-esteem depend on what you think or say to yourself, not what others think or say.

124

Worry Is a Waste of Time

It doesn't change anything or make anything better. As a matter of fact, worrying is like praying for what you don't want because, according to the Law of Attraction, you get more of what you focus on.

Action Plan

When you find yourself worrying or feeling concerned about a situation, get crystal clear *why* are you worrying.

Write it down, including how you feel about it and what power you have to change the situation.

Now *reframe* by asking yourself these questions:

❋ "How can I leverage or capitalize on this situation to turn it around to my benefit?"

❋ "What solutions can remedy the current worrisome situation?"

❋ "Who can I get assistance from?"

❋ "What resources are available that I have not investigated?"

Now, armed with your new data, take some actions toward the worry.

Don't forget to pray and envision the outcome you want.

125

Love Who You Are Right Now

At the end of the day, you are your longest commitment and your own best friend and confidant. It is you that will save you from yourself.

Action Plan

"Make yourself a priority" must be your new motto in these changing and confusing times. Switch off the auto pilot of your old choices and start seeing life and situations from a new perspective.

Give yourself a break!

Forgive yourself for all your past mistakes—and everyone else for theirs who still bother you and take away your peace of mind.

Do something extraordinary that you will be pleased about in the future! Every day is a new day to start again.

126

Never Claim Illness

Never say you are sick, even if you are sick.

Say instead that you are healing.

Words are like powerful seeds.

Once planted, they can bring forth health or disease, success or failure, and happiness or sadness.

Action Plan

Be smart with your language. Realize you personally carry a great responsibility for the words you use. You are a self-fulfilling prophecy, so think yourself well, happy, and successful.

127

Enjoy Little Things in Life

Start today to give yourself permission to sincerely enjoy the little things in life because one day you will look back and realize these small things were actually the big things.

Action Plan

Choose to enjoy being in the now moment of your life.

Stop wishing away your life and *be* in the now!

Enjoy your routines, friendships, and the blessings that come your way.

Remember that, with the blink of an eye, it can all vanish.

Be grateful always, every day.

128

Be Your Authentic Self

The more you wake up to who you are, the more unbearable it will become to be who you are not.

Action Plan

The best part of allowing yourself to be authentic is that you have no image or mask to maintain.

Being your true self will delight some and upset others, and none of it will concern the truth of your being.

You are who you are ... and you have the scars to prove it. Be you!

129

Observe the Ones Who Find True Happiness in Life

They are the ones who don't make excuses.

If it's broken, they fix it.

If it's wrong, they make It right.

Action Plan

The gap between the life you're living and the life you want is called "choices, behaviors, and actions."

130

Claim Your Authenticity

Action Plan

Speak with honesty.

Think with sincerity.

Act with integrity.

Ask yourself, "Who am I really? Am I honest and in integrity with my own authenticity?"

Acknowledge and release social, family, religious, educational, government, and mainstream media indoctrinations. Releasing old programming and questioning it opens your true self so you can see and discern what your own inclinations and desires are clearly. Once you release what you are not, you can claim your true nature.

131

Make the Most Out of Every Day

The people in life who wonder if the glass is half empty or half full miss the point; the glass is refillable. No one has a guarantee there is a tomorrow.

Action Plan

Decide to enjoy your life now.

The secret to being happy is accepting where you are in life and making the most out of every situation possible. Say out loud and often to yourself, "Today I am making the decision to let go of all the things that don't make me happy. I am attracting wonderful new adventures into my life now."

132

Make a Different Choice!

If you want a different outcome, you must make different decisions and actions!

Action Plan

Everything in your life reflects a choice you have made or not made. Not deciding allows others to take charge of your life.

If you want to make better choices and avoid making the same mistakes again, make more decisions based on your past memories and less decisions based on your current emotions. Get sound advice from people who have walked your path, and always listen to your instincts.

133

The Most Powerful Tool You Have

Everything in your life boils down to your choices. There is a field of infinite possibilities around us daily. Every choice opens an infinite number of doors for you and also shuts an infinite number of possible doors.

Action Plan

Your point of power is this moment of time. You can change the direction of your life by making a new choice. It is now and has always been in your own power and in your own hands, heart, and mind.

Claim this power. One year from today, you will either have a year's list of excuses or a year of progress. The choice is all yours today.

134

Be Unavailable to Pain

Make yourself unavailable to absolutely anything in your life and business that no longer serves you.

Action Plan

When you make yourself unavailable to the old pain and insanity, you make space and energy for the better things, people, and new opportunities. Start today by removing people, situations, and things that are no longer for your highest and best good so you can create a future that has left the old pain behind you.

135

Expectations

Awaken each day with the expectation that something wonderful is about to happen. No matter what is happening, remember that it's quite possible things will turn out far better than you could imagine.

Action Plan

Be aware the primary cause of your unhappiness is never the situation but your thoughts about it.

Clean up your own negative pessimistic or victim attitudes by replacing them with thinking about what you are grateful for and what good things could happen.

136

Release the World's Problems

Instead of using your life energy to focus on situations out of your control, shift your attention to situations in which you do have some ability to help yourself and others.

Action Plan

Focus instead on your trust and belief in yourself, so that no matter what happens you will land on your feet.

Understanding what you focus on will expand in your life. Focus on trust, love, abundance, health, freedom, and what you want to show up for you in your future. Pay attention to the energy you sow in the world about what you believe the future will hold, because ... you are programming your future with your thoughts.

137

Situations Are Temporary

Wisdom is understanding that every situation in your life is temporary.

Action Plan

When life is good, make sure you receive it fully by enjoying it.

When life is not good, remember that the situation is temporary and will not last forever; also remember to actively look for the better days that are on their way. Take action on improving whatever you can to find solutions you need and know that life is always changing, and you can affect those changes.

138

You're Not Just a Survivor

Sometimes life will kick you around until you wake up to your own power.

Sooner or later, you'll realize you're not just a survivor. You'll realize you have become a warrior who stands up and stands your ground.

Action Plan

Program yourself to recognize right away when you go into nonbeneficial states of mind, which include the following:

* Victimhood

* Feeling like a failure

* Anxiety or feeling frustrated or angry

* Feeling envious of others

Use your life skills tools to "pattern interrupt" your ego or inner victim that is trying to take charge of your emotions. A great mental tool is to say "No, no, no!" to the negative emotion that can literally ruin your moment, hour, day, week, or life. Then say, "Yes, yes, yes!" to being present and aware that you are stronger than anything life throws in your path.

139

Beliefs

Every successful person in any field of achievement has two strong beliefs:

- ❋ The future has the potential to be much better than the present.

- ❋ I have the inherent power to make it so.

Action Plan

The quality of your mind makes the quality of your life. Your mind is one of the few things you can control. You literally live in your mind, so make sure you are making your inner power station a habitable, pleasant place.

140

Wisdom and Maturity

Being a good person doesn't mean you have to put up with anyone else's misbehavior.

Action Plan

Real wisdom and maturity mean being willing to walk away from people and situations that threaten your peace of mind, self-worth, self-respect, morals, and values without feeling guilty or obligated. Know when it is time to stay and time to leave.

141

The Power of Action

Sometimes the smallest step in the right direction ends up being one of the biggest steps of your life.

Action Plan

Take small steps—tiptoe if you must—but take the steps and always remember that every champion was once a contender who refused to give up.

What steps do you need to take? Start today.

142

Avoid Regrets

It is better to look back on your life and say, "I can't believe I did that!" than to look back on your life with regrets and wish you had not done that.

If you do not go after what you want, you will never have it.

If you don't move forward toward your goals, you will always be in the same place or falling behind.

If you don't ask for what you want, the answer is always no.

Action Plan

Be proactive with a plan and vision of fulfilling your hopes and dreams.

Your future depends on it.

143

Be in the Present Moment

Expectation is the source of all your suffering. Being in the moment means accepting what's happening around you in this very moment without measuring or judging it in your mind based on what you think life should be or how others should act.

Action Plan

Release all expectations since if you expect something and it doesn't come true, then you suffer. Release the blame and victimhood behaviors. Accept it is what it is and make the best of life.

Keep in mind that an unhealed person can find offense in pretty much anything someone does. A healed person understands that the actions of others have absolutely *nothing* to do with them.

144

Let Your Inner Kid Come Out to Play

Take chances for the adventure of life.

Be crazy and fun-loving and let your inner kid out to play.

Stop waiting for the perfect time.

Why? Because right now is the oldest you've ever been and also the youngest you'll ever be again!

Action Plan

Live your fun life today.

Go often to the following:

1. The places that heal you

2. The places that inspire you

3. The people who make you laugh and be silly

4. The timeless version of yourself who loves to have fun

145

Dance with the Unknown

Life goes on … Claim the day!

Whether you choose to move on and take a chance and *dance* with the unknown or stay behind, locked in the past, thinking about what could have been had you been brave enough to believe in yourself, life goes on.

Action Plan

Claim the day!

Whatever you do today, do it with the confidence of a four-year-old in a Batman T-shirt!

146

If You Fail, Never Give Up

The acronym "FAIL." means "first attempt in learning."

Keep in mind that "END" is not the end. "END" means "effort never dies."

If you get a *no* as an answer, "NO" means "next opportunity."

Action Plan

Reframe failing in your mind so that you see it as just *one* of the steps to your future success.

147

Pick Something and Stick to It

Don't keep changing the image or thought of what you want.

You will greatly delay reaching your goals when your creative energy has to keep starting over each time you change your mind and focus.

Action Plan

Be aware there is a certain amount of accumulated energy that has to gather to birth new things. If you are constantly giving your mind new directions, you dilute your ability to achieve your goals. Pick something and stick to it. Yes, daily you can enhance your vision, but keep the core goal clean so you can get results faster.

148

You Are a
Self-Fulfilling Prophecy

What you think and feel about yourself comes true.

If you don't become conscious of your thoughts, you are dooming yourself to be what society or old connections want you to be.

Action Plan

You must train your mind to be stronger than your emotions or else you'll lose yourself in old programming or other influences that are not in your best interest.

149

No Limits for Your Life

There is no rule that says you have to live life like everyone else.

Action Plan

Give yourself permission to simply live a life true to your own nature.

Other people's rules are their making, and you are a sovereign being deciding on your direction and moral compass.

When a brave man or woman takes a stand, the spines of others are stiffened.

150

Manage Your Own Life Energy

Daily, you must take care of *yourself*.

You cannot pour from an empty cup.

The most important thing you can manage is your own energy.

Action Plan

Each day, nurture and replenish every part of yourself mentally, physically, emotionally, and spiritually, so you can continue being a source of goodness to yourself and others.

To manage your energy, you must have clear unbreakable boundaries and a daily self-care regimen.

151

Focus Your Attention

Focus on the outcome you want to experience.

Action Plan

Have great discernment on the thoughts you allow in your mind. The past is over, and the future is not yet here. It is what you focus on and act on today consistently that will impact your future. So control the caliber of information you allow in your mind. Say, "No, no, no!" to the fears, doubts, and insecurities. Envision the future that brings a smile to your face and heart.

152

There Are No Coincidences

Many spiritual teachers say there are no coincidences or accidents in the world.

Nothing is by chance. Everything you're experiencing is a direct manifestation of where you are focusing your attention, consciousness, and life energy.

Action Plan

Give yourself permission to focus your attention, consciousness, and life energy on what you want to manifest in your world. Release all doubts, fears, and worry about your future and trust you are guided to your divine highest and best good.

153

Boost Your Self-Confidence

Wear accessories you assign a symbol to that can really boost your self-confidence or any other type of power characteristic you want to feel and exhibit.

Action Plan

Wear a piece of clothing or jewelry or carry something around that reminds you to be confident. You can assign "traits" to certain items, so it reminds your subconscious to have that trait. For example, you might assign a bracelet to make you feel fearless. Wear that when you want more courage and bravery.

Have fun with assigning meaning to the objects you own.

154

Helping Others

Helping one person might not change the world, but it could change the world for one person. We must all be of service in some way. That means being present with yourself and knowing how to use your life energy to serve yourself and others.

Action Plan

There are many little things you can do that will, in some way, shift others' lives in a positive way. You can help others with your time, resources, and money. Think of your helping efforts as depositing into your own spiritual bank account. What you sow will always come back to you, with interest!

155

Problem Solving

You cannot solve a problem in the same exact frequency in which the problem was created. If you want something different, you must do something different. Don't repeat what you have done before. Remember that the definition of insanity is doing the same things over and over expecting new results. Look at the situation using an entirely new set of lenses.

Action Plan

Ask yourself, "Where are the blessings or opportunities in this current situation?"

Ask your intuition and subconscious to give you some new and different solutions and look and listen for them.

Make sure you write them down to be able to explore these helpful messages.

156

Honor Your Word

The number one cause of strained and broken relationships, whether personal or business, is unrealized expectations when people don't honor their word.

Asking good questions, then setting, confirming, meeting, and managing expectations is one of the master keys to success.

Honoring your own word is essential for trust. Of course, when we find out we cannot do something we promised, we can call, write, and figure out Plan B.

Action Plan

You *must* honor your word. That one thing defines who you really are!

157

The Power of Quiet Reflective Time

Many people seem to have programmed themselves to be afraid of quiet time. I wonder if they are afraid to hear themselves think. When the average person enters a room, they habitually turn on the television, radio, computer, iPad, or smartphone. Many people preserve no quiet time whatsoever in each day, or even each week.

Frankly, if you identify with this, you need to give yourself a reality check and ask yourself why you are not listening to the inner part of yourself. Those smart devices only keep you distracted from what you are really feeling or from productivity and living.

Action Plan

Schedule yourself quiet time to connect with your higher self and get inspiration. This is where you will literally get the fuel to move forward in life. Being in nature is a great place to spend your quiet time and is very important for your mind, body, and soul.

158

The Best Way to Predict the Future Is to Create It

The difference between who you are and who you want to be is what you do. What you focus on expands.

Action Plan

Make a clear, concise decision of exactly what you want, and act as if it is already in your reality. It becomes your next natural step in life.

159

Set Your Own Path

Your speed doesn't matter. Forward is forward.

Everyone has their own inner pace; don't compare yours to anyone else's. You are an original, and you will get to your destination when you are ready.

Action Plan

Design your own life plan. Your aspirations are yours, so carve out some percentage of your productive time for pursuing those goals. Keep in mind, scheduling fifteen- to thirty-minute intervals to work on a small project is very powerful. Once you're done, you have the appetite and confidence for being more productive and getting more projects done! Consider using the word project versus work since that feels like it will be more fun.

160

You Have Free Will to Choose

You have free will, but you are not free from the consequences of your choice and actions.

Action Plan

Decide to evolve and not remain the same as you have always been.

If you decide you want to go back to whatever normal was, you will be presented with the same challenges, the same situations, and the same routine until you grow beyond them and learn from them.

If you decide to evolve, you will align with the core strength inside you, you will become an adventurer, and you will explore new horizons. As you evolve and adapt to what changes are upon us, you will awaken to love for yourself and others. When you choose to evolve, you choose love—the most powerful force in the Universe.

161

Review Your Perceived Rejections

As you look back on your life, do you realize that every time you thought you were being *rejected* from something good ... you were actually being *redirected* to something better?

Action Plan

Reframe your old pain into powerful learning lessons that open you to view your so-called losses, failures, rejections, and betrayals as interventions, saving you from a nonbeneficial future.

162

Your Words

Your words can inspire or destroy someone's dreams, including your own.

Action Plan

Use words wisely. If you don't have anything encouraging to say, maybe just do not say anything, if possible. Your words are just as powerful in everyday use as they are in the hands of professional writers. Let's be encouragers and not discouragers to ourselves and others.

163

Be Very Selective

Hang out with people who fit your future, not your past.

Action Plan

Keep those worth keeping, and, with the breath of kindness, blow the rest away.

Get real with yourself about who is no longer seeing life through the same lens as you and about who you feel tense and drained around.

Get real with yourself about who is in alignment with you right now and about who supports you and your values and morals. If you feel enlivened around them, they are your tribe.

164

Intuition Is Your Superpower

Also known as your instincts or gut feeling, the real reason you have a hard time trusting this inner power is because you still believe that some outside authority knows more and is smarter than you.

Think of all the bad advice you have received from different so-called experts in all areas of life, such as medical, financial, government, education, real estate, insurance, and any other type of business you can think of.

Action Plan

Do not make decisions without your own due diligence, which includes listening to your instincts, and never be afraid to get more than one opinion.

165

Life Timing

Don't wait for the time to be just right because it will never be just right.

Action Plan

Your new motto is "You build your plane while you fly it." This means that when you are completely committed to a project, you can launch the project with the mindset that you will figure it out as you go. No one can accurately predict the future, so embark on the projects and adventures you want to engage in now—stop waiting! It is better to experiment and change course than to never get started.

166

You Are a Collage of Data!

You are the books you read, the movies you watch, the music you listen to, the people you associate with, and all the conversations you engage in.

Action Plan

Choose wisely what you feed your mind and soul daily. You become like what you are connected to. Break away from negative people and negative habits. Love yourself enough to take care of your unrealized future by seeding it with high integrity, energy, and love.

167

Your Present Situation

The best is yet to come in your life, and your present reality is not your final destination.

Action Plan

Always be looking forward to the future with plans and excited anticipation.

Create vision boards, write out your goals, and script daily about your upcoming fantastic adventures!

168

Your Point of Power Is Now

This very moment is your point of power. Life will become more meaningful when you realize the simple fact that you'll never get the same moment twice.

Action Plan

Don't squander your time away; squeeze every drop of joy, fun, and happiness you can out of your life. Don't waste it watching other people's lives on TV or hanging around procrastinators who will never get their act together. Walk away from all distractions that prevent you from realizing your true potential. Your point of power is now: go for what you want.

169

Never Let Anyone Break Your Spirit

———

When people are intimidated by or jealous of your strength, accomplishments, determination, and fortitude, they will try to tear you down and break your spirit.

Action Plan

Remember, it's a reflection of their weakness and *not* a reflection of you. Do not let their poison arrows and their sheer jealousy affect you in any way. Simply observe the true colors of this person and give them the *gift* of your absence.

170

Before You Argue with Anyone

Pause and ask yourself, "Am I using my life energy in an effective manner?" and "Is this person even mentally mature enough to grasp the concept of a different perspective?" If not, you are wasting your time talking to them.

Action Plan

Simply remove yourself from the situation as fast as possible. Do a pattern interrupt to stop the conversation and excuse yourself. Then pat yourself on the back for leaving an unwinnable situation. It is a wise person who walks away from unwinnable games.

171

Why Do I Succeed?

- ❋ I am willing to do the things others are not.
- ❋ I will fight against the odds.
- ❋ I am not controlled by fear, doubts, insecurities, and past mistakes.
- ❋ If I am beaten, I will find a way to return.
- ❋ If I fall down, I will get up.
- ❋ I will always aim to get better, and I will never stop.
- ❋ I will never give up on my personal dreams.

That is why I succeed in waking up every morning with a clear purpose that guides me.

Action Plan

I will never allow external things to make me give up. I have a clear purpose on earth, and I am going to fulfill it.

172

Pay Attention to Signals

Here are some red flags and alarm bells:

* Cheaters always accuse you of cheating.
* Liars always accuse you of lying.
* Insecure people make you feel insecure.

Action Plan

Pay close attention to how people treat you. It reflects who they really are.

Stop giving people chances who have already shown you their ability to manipulate you, and open your eyes to the truth in front of you. Don't waste your time and energy trying to rehabilitate them. Move on and find people who enliven and support you, people you enjoy being with. Life is short—refuse to allow manipulators to control one minute of your time, energy, or frame of mind. Life becomes a lot easier when you move away from people who show you their dark side.

173

Everyone Has Challenges

Everyone has challenges on many levels: mentally, emotionally, physically, spiritually, and financially. To truly heal from your challenges, you must do something extraordinary to break out of old patterns and the feeling of being stuck.

Action Plan

Take an honest look at the role you play in your own suffering. Decide to become unstuck and get help reversing the negative behaviors, attitudes, and beliefs that are contributing to your misfortune so your challenges will, over time, lessen and remove themselves from your life. Choose today to be your day of breaking free of old restrictions.

174

A Cardinal Rule of Life

Never, ever allow anyone to tell you what you can and can't do with your skills, talents, life energy, and future. Prove your detractors wrong. Feel sorry for them because they have no imagination of what is possible for you!

Action Plan

This is your life, and the sky's the limit. This is your blue sky. Now go forth in life, and have a grand adventure!

175

Stop Postponing Your Good Life

The longer you engage in what's not good for you, the longer you postpone what is good for you. Wake up to the fact that you have to make changes to open new possibilities.

Action Plan

You already know the list of what/who is and is not good for you.

Stop pretending you don't know, and invoke some courage to do the right thing for yourself since **no one can save you but you.** You must be the one to take the first step toward becoming the person you were meant to be in life.

176

Old Keys Don't Unlock New Doors

We are living in a new world. Old keys don't unlock new doors, and you must upgrade your life to fit into the new world you want to experience.

Action Plan

Release all things and people that are weighing you down.

Release emotional attachments to the following:

* People

* Material possessions

* Titles and status (ego stuff)

* Old emotional patterns

When you want something different for yourself, you must start moving, thinking, and acting differently. Create new habits of being curious and open minded, looking for opportunities around you. Release what is no longer serving you. By releasing the old, you make room for the new in your life.

177

Help Yourself!

All the advice in the world will never help you until you help yourself!

Action Plan

It's on you to get you to where you want to be. Once you become fearless, life becomes limitless. Step up to the plate and decide once and for all that you deserve to thrive in life; that can start today by shifting your mindset of what is possible and then taking action toward that purpose.

178

Hoping Isn't a Viable Strategy

Sorry to break it to you, but hoping isn't a strategy. Do you have a project that's going nowhere? Go back to square one and reevaluate the situation. Take your power back and stop waiting for someone or something to save you. Be proactive and get real with yourself about what you have done and what you have let slide to your own detriment.

❋ What are the steps you know you should take, but you have not?

❋ What are the steps other "experts" in that field do and recommend that you have not tried?

Action Plan

Accept that there are downsides in all situations and your job is to find a solution, not let your fear paralyze you. Just take that step toward where you want to go. Baby steps are just fine, just go in the direction of your aspirations and once you act, solutions will start to appear for you to consider.

179

What You Are Seeking Is Seeking You

It may show up in a day or a year, but what's meant to be will always find a way.

Action Plan

Your dreams don't have an expiration date. Keep looking for evidence that your dreams will come true. Take inspired action toward the outcomes you seek daily. Be willing to explore opportunities in areas you have not explored before and give yourself some new options and then watch new opportunities start to materialize.

180

Allow Your Natural Self to Emerge

Surrender to your natural self and be yourself, no matter what others think or say.

Action Plan

Be the original you were born to be. Stop being a prisoner of popular opinions, trends, fads, and others insane expectations of how to live your life. The most important cage you can free yourself from is the opinions of others. An original is always worth more than a copy! Set your authentic self free! Just decide to live happily ever after—no matter what!

181

The New Version of You

Transformation to an upgraded you takes time. When making some improvements in your life or work, be willing to go through a phase of feeling uncomfortable and deal with challenging processes. There are no shortcuts to growing into a new version of yourself.

Action Plan

Envision the new, upgraded you in action. *Act* as if you are already the person you are inspired to become.

182

Everyone Starts off as a Novice

The expert in anything was once a beginner. Success is nothing more than chosen disciplines, practiced every day. Three months from now, you will either have three months of excuses or three months of progress. The choice is always yours.

Action Plan

Stop comparing your life book's first chapter to someone else's Chapter 20. Daily look for your improvements and advances.

183

Discernment

Make yourself unavailable to absolutely anything that doesn't serve you.

Action Plan

When you make yourself unavailable to the drama, misbehavior, and nonsense, you make space for better things, people, and opportunities. Train your mind to discern what is beneficial and what is not beneficial to your life, and act on your instincts.

184

Decide to Be a Leader

It only takes one light to illuminate the darkness.

Action Plan

Never underestimate the light you shine into the world. Your energy in all situations makes a difference. Stand up for your convictions and be a good example in all your actions.

185

Leave the Table of Disrespect

Head's up: you can't keep getting angry at folks for sucking the life out of you if you keep giving them the straw.

Action Plan

You must learn to get up from the table when respect for you is no longer being served. You can't change someone or an organization who doesn't see an issue with their negative behaviors and actions. You can only change how you react to them or move on and find people and situations that are better suited to you personally.

186

Find Courage to Break Old Patterns

Decide to bring forth within you the courage to break the patterns in your life that are no longer serving you.

Action Plan

It is not hard to change when you understand the cost of staying the same. Courage is looking fear right in the eye and saying, "Get the Hell out of my way; I've got things to do."

Courage doesn't mean you don't get afraid. Courage means you don't let fear stop you from going for your heart's desires or the right thing. End the fear of what could go wrong by shifting your thoughts to start being excited about what could go right. Start to focus on what you want in life versus what you do not want.

187

Stop Trying to Calm the Storm

Action Plan

Calm yourself first. The primary cause of our unhappiness is not the situation but your thoughts about it.

The storm will pass. It is quite possible things will turn out far better than you could imagine. You make better decisions in a calm, unemotional state of mind.

188

Delight in the Best of Life

Use and enjoy your best things!

Enjoy your jewelry, fancy clothes, best china, expensive pens, and the best of everything you own. Nowadays, just being alive is a special occasion.

Action Plan

Break out your good stuff and delight in the best of your life. Have a good time!

189

Life Always Offers You More Chances

It's called tomorrow morning.

The gaps between the life you're living and the life you sincerely want are called choices and actions.

Action Plan

Make better choices and take action to live a better life.

190

Pave Your Own Path

When you know what you want, go for it with relentless work and determination!

Action Plan

Keep your plans to yourself, and never tell anyone who is not a true supporter of your pursuit. Their jealousy can discourage you from believing in your own dream. It is better to show people what you are going to do rather than tell them in advance.

191

Be Scared and Do It Anyway

There is no passion to be found in playing small or settling for a life that is less than the one you are capable of living. Comfort is the enemy of serious, life-changing growth.

Action Plan

Be scared and do it anyway. Be underqualified and get in the game anyway. Be unsure, imperfect, and messy but show up anyway.

Accept the phase of being uncomfortable, for this too shall pass with time and effort.

Life is simply too precious and short not to live full out in ways that empower you.

192

Challenging Times

There will always be challenging times and times of transition in your life. Challenges make us stronger and more resilient.

Action Plan

Remember that obstacles can't stop you. Problems can't stop you. People can't stop you. Only you can stop you.

Repeat to yourself daily, "*No matter the circumstances, I always end up on top!*"

193

Focus on the Solutions

The more you focus on the solution instead of the problem, the more peaceful and successful your life becomes. Life is so much brighter when you focus on what truly matters to you!

Action Plan

State to yourself daily, "I choose to have magic and miracles in my life!"

Sometimes the smallest step toward the solution you want ends up being the biggest step of your life. Take baby steps if needed but make a move.

194

You Cannot Pour from an Empty Vessel

Action Plan

You must regularly replenish mentally, physically, emotionally, and spiritually so as not to burn out. Update, refresh, and restart your brain as many times as you need to. It works just like a computer so make sure you're the only one programming it. Give yourself permission to rest when needed, fuel your body with foods that enliven it, and feed your soul with the beauty of nature.

195

Break Up with Being Normal

Give yourself permission to stop valuing being normal, and it will be the first day of your new life.

Action Plan

Give yourself permission to spread your wings to go on adventures to find out where you truly belong! Being normal is not necessarily a virtue ... It rather denotes a lack of courage.

196

Your Quest for Personal Growth

The greatest gift we can offer to others is the personal growth we offer to ourselves.

Action Plan

Decide to become a contributor of goodness in the world. Offer encouragement where needed. Choose to be a light in the darkness. Be an example of a good human, leader, neighbor, friend, spouse, and parent. The World needs all the positive, empowering examples it can get! Change must start with you taking responsibility for your own personal growth.

197

You Are Evolving

Stop shrinking yourself to fit places you've outgrown.

Life has evolved, and you cannot go back to the old "normal." You have outgrown that life. That means some "jobs," people, traditions, and attitudes need to be reevaluated and updated to the new you and your new future.

Action Plan

Embrace the new life you are creating right now. Take an active part in designing your own destiny. Appreciate and accept that you have moved on as a natural part of your evolving in life. Time to spread your wings and fly into the new future!

198

Remove Toxic Energy

Eliminate all the toxic emotions from your mental diet and watch your health and life improve.

Action Plan

Stop chewing on worry, guilt, blame, anger, regret, and resentment! Just let it all go and now focus on finding and enacting on new solutions.

199

Feeling Discouraged

Here is what to tell yourself when your situation has you feeling discouraged:

1. This situation is tough, but so am I.

2. I may not be able to control this current situation, but I can control how I react to it.

3. I haven't figured out what to do about this yet, but I will.

4. I am determined to land on my feet!

Action Plan

Examine your discouraging situation from all sides, then take one corrective step at a time to move your emotional energy from discouraging to encouraging.

200

Never Be Ruled by What Others Think of You

Action Plan

Don't let people's compliments go to your head and don't let their criticisms go to your heart. The degree to which you do either of these things is the degree to which you will be ruled by what other people think of you. Become a sovereign being. What you think of yourself is the most important opinion.

201

Real Courage Means Embracing the Unknown

Action Plan

Be brave! Be bold! It takes courage to do anything that's different from what you normally do. You just might like what you see when the unknown becomes known. Be willing to take risks and venture into the unknown and unexplored. Life should be treated like a grand adventure and experiment. How do you know what you like if you don't try new things?

202

Choose to Focus Only on Your Next Step in Life

Trying to envision your entire path and how it will work out will only delay you from taking the next, immediate step you need to take.

Action Plan

Do what is in front of you that needs to be done and stop worrying about trying to know every step of your future. By focusing on your next step, the future literally shifts to what you are focused on, revealing your entire path one next step at a time.

203

Get Out of Feeling Entitled in Any Level of Your Life

There is no rule that says you should always be dealt a great hand in the poker game of life.

Action Plan

Play the hell out of the cards you are holding right now, even if they stink. Capitalize on your current knowledge, talents, skills, and wisdom. A good bluffer can make everyone at the table fold, even if they're holding aces.

204

Don't Be Afraid to Fail

Be Afraid *not* to start. Don't die with your music still in you. Embrace the experience of failing as just a stepping stone to your destination.

Action Plan

Procrastination can be eliminated with just the slightest movement toward what you want. Any speed toward your goals is better than standing still, but whatever your 100 percent looks like, give it!

205

Real Success Comes When You Refuse to Give Up!

Excuses will turn your dreams into dust. Make your personal goals so strong and so important to you that any failure, obstacle, or loss now only acts as motivation on your path to greatness.

Action Plan

Make success inevitable by surrounding yourself with people who illuminate your path, who push you to dig deeper and never give up, and who support you even in challenging times. Those are your people.

206

Catching People Doing Things Right!

Get out of the negative habit of being a fault finder— to yourself and others. Replace the negative behavior of fault finding with the new habit of catching people doing things right!

Action Plan

Compliment people. Magnify their strengths, not their weaknesses. Be a *hope* dealer in life, not a *nope* dealer!

207

Ready to Up Your Game?

To achieve goals you have not achieved before, you must become someone you have not been before. You've got a new story to write, and it looks nothing like your past story. You must do things to up your game like becoming a student of something that will propel you forward, joining a high-end mastermind group, getting a coach, or anything that holds you accountable.

Action Plan

Act from the perspective that nothing can stop the hero of your new story (you) from becoming what you focus on and work toward because giving up is not an option for heroes!

208

Magnet for Miracles

A grateful heart is a magnet for miracles. Gratitude is the highest vibration that exists—it's even higher than love.

Action Plan

Happiness is not about getting all you want; it is about enjoying all you have. Acknowledge daily what you are truly grateful for by writing out a list every day of your blessings. The more blessings you acknowledge, the more blessings you will attract! There is no other emotion more powerful than gratitude to shift any situation.

209

Age Is No Barrier
to Achievement

Your age is a limitation people put in their own minds. If you think you're too young or too old to do anything, think again! If there is a will, there's a way.

Action Plan

Watch yourself talk about what you think you can and cannot do in life. For inspiration, research who is the oldest person who has achieved what it is you desire to do. Decide to defy norms and go for whatever is calling you to achieve.

210

Trust Yourself First

The most destructive thing you can do to yourself is believe someone else's opinion of you, especially if they wish you harm or don't believe in you.

Action Plan

Avoiding "certain" people to protect your emotional health is not a weakness; it is wisdom.

211

Worrying Is Praying for What You Don't Want

Action Plan

Let go of what you think your life is supposed to look like and focus on believing in yourself. There is no such thing as failure, only results. When you find yourself worrying, do a pattern interrupt on yourself and stop those thoughts and start asking, "What is the solution to this problem? Who could help or guide me to a good outcome?" Focus on new solutions and not the old problem. What you focus on always expands so train yourself to focus on what you want.

212

Align Yourself with Your New Future

Action Plan

As your life changes, so will your world.

Make new choices that are aligned with exactly who you are now and the future you want to seed.

If it doesn't make you feel great, follow this advice:

❋ **Don't do it.**

❋ **Don't buy it.**

❋ **Don't keep it.**

Release all guilt and obligations since that energy derails you from the future you seek.

213

Who Will Change Your Destiny?

If you are still looking for that one person who will change your life ...

Action Plan

Look in the mirror.

You must be willing to take 100 percent responsibility for your own actions, behaviors, and attitudes. No one will love you or betray you more than yourself. Own the truth that you must be the one coming to save you.

214

Dedicated to Helping Yourself

All the advice in the world can't help you until you help yourself.

Beware that obstacles are what you will see when you take your eyes off your goals.

Action Plan

Stop waiting for the perfect time or the perfect situation to get started on a project. Take action! Once you have started, notice how what you need to do next seems to organically appear before you.

BONUS PRAYERS

From Lee Milteer's book *The Magic of Prayers: 70
Powerful Prayers to Manifest What You Desire*
Available on Amazon

Direction and Guidance

Dear Universe:

Please assist me to hear your divine guidance. Direct me to use my life energy in the most productive, profitable, and spirit-directed ways. Give me confidence and faith to know that I am connected to you and to all life.

I know that I am always under the direct inspiration of Infinite Intelligence. I make right decisions easily and effortlessly. So be it.

Thank you. Amen.

Goal-Driven Behavior

Dear Creator:

I am now one with Source. Infinite Intelligence is filling me with the power to define, clarify, and carry through with exactly the right and perfect goals for my life.

I now pursue only those goals about which I have received clarity and direction from Infinite Intelligence.

With Infinite Intelligence as my partner, I have all the energy, focus, and right ideas I need to succeed in my goals. So be it.

Thank you. Amen.

Visionary Insight

Dear Heavenly Mother and Father:

Guide me today to delicately steer my thoughts and images in my mind's eye to those that are aligned with my divine purpose. Allow me to be inspired to create peace, harmony, perfect health, happiness, prosperity, love, and well-being in my life.

Assist me to see myself as one who is filled with vitality, good health, confidence, creativity, and enthusiasm for my life and work. Allow me to work out any "challenges" in the workshop of my mind and to see the perfect solutions as they come to me through intuition.

Thank you for my daily guidance and for always leading me to my highest and best good. So be it.

Thank you. Amen.

ABOUT LEE MILTEER

For a full bio for Lee Milteer, please visit her website at www.milteer.com.

Lee Milteer is an internationally known best-selling author, award-winning professional speaker, visionary, TV personality, and intuitive business mentor and serial entrepreneur.

Lee is a performance and mastery of success coach, and she has counseled, trained, mentored, and spoken in live events to more than a million people all over North America, Japan, and Europe in conventions, private companies, and entrepreneurial and niche market events.

She hosted the *America's Premier Experts* TV show, which was aired on NBC, CBS, ABC, and Fox affiliates, as well as *Untamed Success: Positive TV*, a web-based TV show. Lee hosted two talk shows in Virginia and was part of an international talk ensemble national TV show in Canada.

As president of Lee Milteer, Inc., Career Development Strategists, she has counseled and trained in organizations such as Ford Motor Co., NASA, Federal Express, Walt Disney, AT&T, XEROX, IBM, 3M, and Sales & Marketing Executive International. Hundreds of government agencies and scores of conventions, associations, meetings, and niche market events repeatedly retain her to inspire and motivate their audiences.

Lee is a recognized, award-winning, best-selling audio and video author. Lee has written five best-selling books, including *Reclaim the Magic, The Magic of Prayers, Success Is an Inside Job, Spiritual Power Tools for Successful Selling,* and *Women Who Mean Business.*

Lee has also coauthored nine more books, including *Renegade Millionaire* with Dan S. Kennedy. Lee's training courses are translated into Japanese, Russian, Dutch, French, Italian, Spanish, and other languages.

Lee has been an expert guest on more than 1,400 shows and podcasts on national and international TV and radio. Lee has been interviewed in hundreds of newspapers, magazines, and trade journals all over the world, including *USA TODAY,* the *Wall Street Journal,* and *INC magazine.*

She is the founder of the Millionaire Smarts Coaching program, which supplies coaching for other coaches and businesses, plus the host of the virtual coaching mentoring program Club for Entrepreneurs.

For more information on Lee Milteer, such as how you could become part of one of Lee's one-on-one coaching programs or use Millionaire Smarts Life and Business Mastery Programs in your business, or to have her speak at your event, please visit www.milteer.com.

LEE MILTEER'S RESOURCES

It's free! Subscribe to Lee Milteer's Gems of Wisdom weekly newsletter. www.milteer.com

It's free! Subscribe to Lee Milteer's Five Types of Energy video series

to learn about your five types of energy (mental, emotional, financial, physical, and spiritual) and how to use your life energy more effectively. To sign up, go to **www.fivetypesofenergy.com**

To join Lee Milteer's Club for Entrepreneurs, Business Owners & Creatives, please visit www.milteer.com and look under coaching.

For more information about Lee Milteer's one-on-one coaching sessions, speaking dates (nationally and internationally), Vision Quests retreats, VIP days, and private business mentoring or to have her speak to your event or podcast or to interview her about this book, go to **www.milteer.com**

Printed in the USA
CPSIA information can be obtained
at www.ICGtesting.com
JSHW022211140824
68134JS00018B/995

9 781642 257342